DELIVERANCE HANDBOOK

- Getting Free Jesus' Way -

ANTHONY SLUZAS

DELIVERANCE HANDBOOK

- Getting Free Jesus' Way -

Anthony Sluzas

ISBN: 1677754834
13-Digit: 978-1677754830

Printed in the United States of America.

Cover, interior design, and editing by:
The Righteous Pen Publications Group
The righteousness of God shall guide my pen
www.righteouspenpublications.com

FOR WE DO NOT WRESTLE AGAINST
FLESH AND BLOOD,
BUT AGAINST PRINCIPALITIES,
AGAINST POWERS,
AGAINST THE RULERS OF THE DARKNESS OF
THIS AGE,
AGAINST SPIRITUAL *HOSTS*
OF WICKEDNESS
IN THE HEAVENLY *PLACES.*
(**E**PHESIANS 6:12)

10-19-2021

Brother Morris +
Sister Angela!

Thanks so much for
blessing my ministry so
greatly. Enjoy the books!
I love y'all. God bless you

Tony Suarez

TABLE OF CONTENTS

CHAPTER ONE

DELIVERANCE

**STAND FAST THEREFORE IN THE LIBERTY
BY WHICH CHRIST HAS MADE
US FREE, AND DO NOT BE ENTANGLED
AGAIN WITH A YOKE OF BONDAGE.
(GALATIANS 5:1)**

The genuine ministry of deliverance

Let's begin by focusing on the deliverance of a believer in Jesus Christ. Yes, many Christians are in need of deliverance, even after being saved from the "clinging vines of the fall upon humankind." We first need to understand that there are different realms of deliverance, such as physical, emotional, and mental. We then must, prayerfully and boldly, confront the bondage or addiction in the power of the Spirit of God, the truth of the Word of God, and the blood of Jesus. The delivering power of Jesus Christ is a continual liberating process in the life of a believer. It is the power of the finished work of the Cross in action, and it's an ongoing process. The Lord desires that we experience the full and total deliverance from our old way of life and walk in the victory of the Cross.

When we approach the subject of deliverance, we're talking about everything that the Lord Jesus Christ does when a person comes to Him to be saved. From the time we are born again until we leave this world to be with Him in heaven, these different dimensions are part of His deliverance program. The cross of Christ has made provision for every form of deliverance we could ever need; spirit, soul, body, financially, and socially. When we refer to the Cross, we are not talking about that literal wooden beam on which Jesus died; but rather, what He there accomplished for all humankind. The great price of our deliverance was the shedding of His life's blood, bearing our sin and punishment. The proof of our deliverance is in His resurrection. Jesus says that because He lives, we will live also. The life that He invites us into brings us victory over every expression of death. We're now completely accepted and viewed as righteous and holy in the sight of God, and it's all because of Jesus.

It's important to keep in mind that God calls us to progressive growth. This doesn't take place without a progressive process of deliverance. Throughout every believer's life, we absolutely do get attacked by the dark works of the enemy, here on earth. If a believer so chooses, he or she can submit to these attacks (either out of ignorance or disobedience). When you continually allow the enemy to have a place in a particular area, the nature of that particular bondage moves beyond your flesh (self) to a stronghold of the enemy deep within the soul (mind, will, and emotions).

It's time we put on the "new man." In Paul's letter to the Ephesians 4:17-32, the apostle begins a series of very practical instructions...

This I say, therefore, and testify in the Lord, that you should no longer walk as the rest of the Gentiles walk, in the futility of their mind, having their understanding darkened, being alienated from the life of God, because of the ignorance that is in them, because of the blindness of their heart; who, being past feeling, have given themselves over to lewdness, to work all uncleanness with greediness.

But you have not so learned Christ, if indeed you have heard Him and have been taught by Him, as the truth is in Jesus: that you put off, concerning your former conduct, the old man which grows corrupt according to the deceitful lusts, and be renewed in the spirit of your mind, and that you put on the new man which was created according to God, in true righteousness and holiness.

Therefore, putting away lying, "Let each one of you speak truth with his neighbor, for we are members of one another. "Be angry, and do not sin:" do not let the sun go down on your wrath, nor give place to the devil. Let him who stole steal no longer, but rather let him labor, working with his hands what is good, that he may have something to give him who has need. Let no corrupt word proceed out of your mouth, but what is good for necessary edification, that it may impart grace to the hearers. And do not grieve the Holy Spirit of God, by Whom you were sealed for the day of redemption. Let all bitterness, wrath, anger, clamor, and evil speaking be put away from you, with all malice. And be kind to one another, tenderhearted, forgiving one another, even as God in Christ forgave you.

Here the Apostle Paul points out specific things to which believers should not submit themselves. He tells us that since we've come into this new and living way with Jesus, we shouldn't and don't have to walk in the ways of a dark and sinful world anymore. We haven't learned this way of life (sensual carnality) in Christ. He wants us to cast off the old sin nature corrupted by deceitful lusts. Understand that lust isn't exclusively about illicit sex; it is the quest for control. Lust is any mode of selfishness (wanting whatever you want whenever you want it) and disregarding anyone else, and the consequences of personal actions.

Paul encourages us to be renewed in the spirit of our minds and to put on the new man. He goes on to explain a whole set of things that characterize "the flesh" (i.e. stealing, anger, bitterness, slothfulness, etc.). When you're deciding whether to put on the new man or the old man, you will either give place to the Spirit of the living God, or to the wicked one.

It's very important to keep in mind there are two realms of deliverance: psychological (the soul) or physical healing. Psychological deliverance includes mental and emotional liberation. When we repeatedly give place to the devil, there comes a point of control given over to Satan in our personalities. This becomes a manipulative entry point of the enemy, where he can then manipulate, restrict, and torment us.

Let's take a look at some varied reactions to deliverance in the Bible. In Mark's Gospel, verses 1:21-27, Jesus cast out a demon from a believer. Many people thought this was a new form of teaching. Let's examine this.

Then they went into Capernaum, and immediately on the Sabbath He entered the synagogue and taught. And they were astonished at His teaching, for He taught them as one having authority, and not as the scribes.

Now there was a man in their synagogue with an unclean spirit. And he cried out, saying, "Let us alone! What have we to do with You, Jesus of Nazareth? Did You come to destroy us? I know Who You are – the Holy One of God!"

But Jesus rebuked him, saying, "Be quiet, and come out of him!" And when the unclean spirit had convulsed him and cried out with a loud voice, he came out of him. Then they were all amazed, so that they questioned among themselves, saying, "What is this? What new doctrine is this? For with authority He commands even the unclean spirits, and they obey Him."

Religious people sometimes think the same thing when they hear the word "deliverance." In Mark 3:22-30, the religious people thought Jesus' ministry of deliverance was satanic. You'll find religionists today that call the work of deliverance by the Holy Spirit "demonic" and that's dangerous—for those making such accusations.

And the scribes who came down from Jerusalem said, "He has Beelzebub," and, "By the ruler of the demons He casts out demons."

So, He called them to Himself and said to them in parables: "How can Satan cast out Satan? If a kingdom is divided against itself, that kingdom cannot stand. And if a house is divided against itself, that house cannot stand. And if Satan has risen up against himself, and is divided, he cannot stand, but has an end. No one can enter a strong man's house and plunder his goods, unless he first binds the strong man. And then he will plunder his house.

"Assuredly, I say to you, all sins will be forgiven the sons of men, and whatever blasphemies they may utter; but he who blasphemes against the Holy Spirit never has forgiveness, but is subject to eternal condemnation"— because they said, "He has an unclean spirit."

Let's briefly talk about points of bondage and being made free.

- The Holy Spirit will reveal points of bondage already in us. Some points of serious bondage will need immediate attention through the help of mature believers such as our pastor, elders, church leaders, or a close friend. Other points of bondage we will outgrow. By and large, we know that people want to be free from bondages and they want to know a center of ministry that can help bring freedom to their lives.

- There are types of bondage of which we will need to have a clearer picture as to what it is we're dealing with. There is a definite distinction between demonic possession and bondage in the life of a believer. Demonic possession takes place at the spirit level. I cannot stress the following fact strongly enough: A believer cannot be demon possessed, because his or her spirit belongs to Christ. An evil spirit or demon can't penetrate the blood of Jesus on the spirit of a believer.

However, a believer can be oppressed, give sway, and submit to demonic bondage in a particular area(s) of their lives.

- There are levels of deliverance in four specific areas. There's deliverance from sin, self, sickness, and Satan. Ephesians 6:12 says our battle isn't with flesh and blood. Our battles are not with people. Behind the battles that we face are much larger issues. Behind everything is a governing spirit. The Bible teaches us that there are three types of spirits operating in the world today: there is the Holy Spirit, then the human spirit, and a hellish spirit. The issues we deal with are spiritual. The music we listen to as well as the movies and media we watch, what we read, the way we conduct ourselves in conversation, and the habits we allow into our lives are all driven by either the Holy Spirit, our own spirit, or unholy spirits.

To be sure, there is a spiritual wrestling match going on in all these things. Satan and his minions viciously attack humans so he can gain a foothold and a place in a believer's life. Since he cannot get the person's spirit, the adversary wants to weigh us down. The fiery arrows of the evil one can penetrate to create points of bondage in the mind and life of a believer.

One of the main reasons why people get trapped into bondage is because of ignorance. Isaiah 5:13 says:

...my people have gone into captivity because they have no knowledge...

There's power in the Word of God! We need to grow in the truth because it will set us free (John 8:32). The Word of God points out what's in the soul and what's in the spirit of a man or woman. The Word is powerful enough to set us free and release us from any evil spirit that would try to hold us down.

We can also get delivered from bondage by the ministry of love. 1 John 4:18 says:

...perfect love casts out fear.

You see, fear terrorizes and exploits all of us at one time or another in life. When we're talking about fear, we're talking about the things that create entire patterns of dishonesty in our lives.

These are masks we wear and façades we put on in order to make ourselves look good to others. We learn to lean on false points of strength because fear tries to break in to our hearts and minds so much. The Bible reassures us that the great love of God is poured into our hearts by the Holy Spirit (Romans 5:5). It's also shown to us by the love, acceptance, and affirmation we receive from other believers.

Another way we receive deliverance is through Holy Spirit-filled and anointed prayer. When we're functioning obediently in the realm of the Holy Spirit, we are called to minister to other believers in bondage (Ephesians 6:1-2). When we walk in the Spirit we can experience deliverance as well. Take time to read through Romans 8:1-15. This passage speaks of life in the Holy Spirit. We are to stand strong and immovable in the liberty that Christ has given us, and not be entangled again by a yoke of slavery (Galatians 5:25). When we walk in the Spirt, we grow in the freedom Christ brings us because of His finished work at the cross. We also experience deliverance by word of authority. Mark 5:8 speaks of the Lord casting out evil spirits with an authoritative word, and we can do the same in Jesus' Name.

The main objective of this little book is to educate believers to different types of bondage, how they can happen, and how they can be set free from them. As we put our faith in the Cross of Christ, grow in the truth of God's Word, get filled with His love, and walk in the Holy Spirit, we receive greater freedom. It is our heavenly Father's desire for each and every one of us to walk in progressive liberty as we mature in Christ and His love.

The nature of spiritual bondage

But in a great house there are not only vessels of gold and silver, but also of wood and clay, some for honor and some for dishonor. Therefore, if anyone cleanses himself from the latter, he will be a vessel of honor, sanctified and useful for the Master, prepared for every good work. Flee also youthful lusts; but pursue righteousness, faith, love, peace with those who call on the Lord out of a pure heart. But avoid foolish and ignorant disputes, knowing that they generate strife. And a servant of the Lord must not quarrel but be gentle to all, able to teach, patient, in humility correcting those who are in opposition, if God perhaps will grant them

repentance, so that they may know the truth, and that they may come to their senses and escape the snare of the devil, having been taken captive by him to do his will.
(2 Timothy 2:20-26)

In this passage of the New Testament, we want to examine Paul's exhortation to Timothy to discover areas of deliverance, entry points to sundry bondages, the pathway of freedom and the instruments of deliverance. Paul calls upon young Timothy to purge himself of those things that hinder him from becoming a vessel of honor to the Lord. He further challenges him to flee youthful lusts. Most of what is problematic to people as adults reaches all the way back to their youth.

There are four basic areas where we need deliverance:

- **Deliverance from sin (Romans 6:23)** – This deliverance takes place when we give our heart to Jesus and are born again. We were dead to sin, but brought back to life through repentance and receiving Jesus Christ as Savior and Lord.

- **Deliverance from the flesh (Self) (Romans 6:6-11)** – The essence of the flesh (self) is to disobey and avoid growth. However, we are delivered from this self-life through Jesus perfecting us when He died on the cross and rose again.

- **Deliverance from sickness and disease (Genesis 2)** – We are vulnerable to sickness because of the fall of humankind. Thankfully, Jesus provided victory over sickness and disease—bringing healing to the whole man.

- **Deliverance from the evil one (Romans 6:17-20)** – Satanic bondage is manifested in a person stampeded or driven into certain behaviors, or as it is walled up and hidden away inside. It puts us into chains of slavery, and inability to overcome in our own power.

There are four areas that can be entry points for the enemy to bring bondage:

- **Great disappointment** – This can become a direct entry point designed to snare us.

Great disappointments can cause people to become bitter and never trust anyone or be vulnerable again. When we are not able to be truly loving and open to God and others, we cause an atmosphere for there to be no room for fulfillment and trust. It breeds unavailability and a lack of credibility in our personality.

- **Divorce and death** – These two traumatic events can register bondage through unforgiveness within your soul. A person in this situation may tend to feel guilty that they never did something they think they should have, or that somehow they were responsible in some way. People learn to build a hard shell around those things and navigate through life without ever confronting them. It breeds an aura of "aloofness" or "standoffishness" in your life toward others, and no credibility to yourself.

- **Deviant behavior** – can give entry to a spirit that can snare or hook a child and bring torment. The enemy has deceived and sandbagged people into living under a lie that tells them they are something they're not.

- **Biological changes or accidents** – We have placed certain expectations on events in life that open a door and give place to the devil. For example, someone might expect a child to rebel at a certain age, or a woman might expect to have a nervous breakdown during pregnancy or menopause. If it actually does happen, we're kind of proud we "prophesied" it. How husbands, family members, and friends respond to women during these times also can open a door and give way to spiritual and physical bondages.

There is a pathway to freedom

No matter what areas we are experiencing bondages, God has a pathway to freedom:

- **We must grow in truth**

    And you shall know the truth, and the truth shall make you free. (John 8:32)

- **There's the ministry of love**

  There is no fear in love; but perfect love casts out fear, because fear involves torment. But he who fears has not been made perfect in love. (1 John 4:18)

- **There's the word of authority**

  He commanded them to take nothing for the journey except a staff – no bag, no bread, no copper in their money belts – but to wear sandals, and not to put on two tunics.

  Also, He said to them, "In whatever place you enter a house, stay there till you depart from that place. And whoever will not receive you nor hear you, when you depart from there, shake off the dust under your feet as a testimony against them. Assuredly, I say to you, it will be more tolerable for Sodom and Gomorrah in the day of judgment than for that city!"

  So, they went out and preached that people should repent. And they cast out

many demons, and anointed with oil many who were sick, and healed them.
(Mark 6:8-12)

- **We're to walk in the Spirit**

   Stand fast therefore in the liberty by which Christ has made us free, and do not be entangled again with a yoke of bondage.
   (Galatians 5:1)

- **Experiencing restoration**

   Brethren, if a man is overtaken in any trespass, you who are spiritual restore such a one in a spirit of gentleness, considering yourself lest you also be tempted. Bear one another's burdens, and so fulfill the law of Christ.
   (Galatians 6:1-2).

Instruments of deliverance

God provides deliverance and freedom through certain instruments:

- **The blood of the cross**

Having wiped out the handwriting of requirements that was against us, which was contrary to us. And He has taken it out of the way, having nailed it to the cross. (Colossians 2:14)

And I, brethren, when I came to you, did not come with excellence of speech or of wisdom declaring to you the testimony of God. For I determined not to know anything among you except Jesus Christ and Him crucified. I was with you in weakness, in fear, and in much trembling. And my speech and my preaching were not with persuasive words of human wisdom, but in demonstration of the Spirit and of power, that your faith should not be in the wisdom of men but in the power of God. However, we speak wisdom among those who are mature, yet not the wisdom of this age, nor of the rulers of this age, who are coming to nothing. But we speak the wisdom of God in a mystery, the hidden wisdom which God ordained before the ages for our glory, which none of the rulers of this age knew; for had they known, they would not have crucified the

Lord of glory. But as it is written: "Eye has not seen, nor ear heard, nor have entered into the heart of man the things which God has prepared for those who love Him," but God has revealed them to us through His Spirit. For the Spirit searches all things, yes, the deep things of God.
(1 Corinthians 2:1-10)

- **The Name of Jesus**

"And these signs will follow those who believe: In My Name they will cast out demons; they will speak with new tongues; they will take up serpents; and if they drink anything deadly, it will by no means hurt them; they will lay hands on the sick, and they will recover." (Mark 16:17-18)

- **The Word of God**

Above all, taking the shield of faith so that you will be able to quench all the fiery darts of the wicked one. (Ephesians 6:16)

- **The flow of the Spirit**

On the last day, that great day of the feast, Jesus stood and cried out, saying, "If anyone thirsts, let him come to Me and drink. He who believes in Me, as the Scripture has said, out of his heart will flow rivers of living water." But this He spoke concerning the Spirit, Whom those believing in Him would receive; for the Holy Spirit was not yet given, because Jesus was not yet glorified.
(John 7:37-39)

"This is the word of the Lord to Zerubbabel: 'Not by might nor by power, but by My Spirit,' says the Lord of Hosts."
(Zechariah 4:6)

- **The gifts of the Spirit**

  1 Corinthians, Chapters 12, 13, 14

- **The Spirit of Praise**

  2 Chronicles 20

- **The song of rejoicing**

For this cause everyone who is godly shall pray to You in a time when You may be found; Surely in a flood of great waters they shall not come near him. You are my hiding place; You shall preserve me from trouble; You shall surround me with songs of deliverance. Selah. (Psalm 32:6-7)

Truth be told, loved one, we all have areas of bondage in our lives that need cleansing and deliverance. The first step is to come to Jesus Christ by acknowledging your need for deliverance and invite Him to begin the work. He will purify us and make us vessels of honor for His glory.

CHAPTER TWO

MINISTRY OF DELIVERANCE

The Lord gives freedom to the prisoners.
(Psalm 146:7)

<u>The flight from evil</u>

This chapter focuses liberation from things that became points of bondage in our youth ("fleeing youthful lusts"). When we see the truth of our present life situation in the Word of God, we can be delivered from things that enslave us. There are many entry points for bondage to take hold: childhood, pregnancy and tragedy, to name a few. When we are finally able to pinpoint the place where that particular bondage began, and then dispel the lie with the Word of God, we will be made free.

The Bible exhorts us to "flee youthful lusts" and to "become a vessel of honor." In 2 Timothy 2:19-26, as is found above, the Apostle Paul talks about a purging process in believers:

Nevertheless, the solid foundation of God stands, having this seal: "The Lord knows those who are His," and "Let everyone who names the Name of Christ depart from iniquity." But in a great house there are not only vessels of gold and silver, but also of wood and clay, some for honor and some for dishonor. Therefore, if anyone cleanses himself from the latter, he will be a vessel for honor, sanctified and useful for the Master, prepared for every good work. Flee also youthful lusts; but pursue righteousness, faith, love, peace with those who call on the Lord out of a pure heart. But avoid foolish and ignorant disputes, knowing that they generate strife. And a servant of the Lord must not quarrel but be gentle to all, able to teach, patient, in humility correcting those who are in opposition, if God perhaps will grant them repentance, so that they may know the truth, and that they may come to their senses and escape the snares of the devil, having been taken captive by him to do his will.

There's a clear recovery process outlined in this passage. It is a flight from evil, characterizing all those who trust in Jesus. The Lord Jesus knows when you're His and established in His life and grace (2 Timothy 2:19). There's a command here that when we become part of the body of Christ, we are to depart from iniquity. In 2 Timothy 2:20, we read there's a great house with vessels of honor and some of dishonor. It doesn't say that any of those dishonorable ones are predestined to always be dishonorable. If there's anything unclean or dishonorable about the vessel, if that person will purge himself, he will become a vessel of honor.

The purging process itself involves expelling anything that would cause life to be dishonorable. This purging process comes by discipline, self-denial, and reckoning ourselves dead unto sin. 2 Timothy 2:22 says to:

"flee also youthful lusts; but pursue righteousness, faith, love, peace, with those who call on the Lord out of a pure heart."

The term, "youthful lusts," has to do with things we encounter that are related to immaturity. These might be things that became bondage points in our childhood and adolescence. The word "lust" has to do with a point of control being secured in our life. Every last one of us have points of control from our youth that we need to "flee" in Jesus' Name. These are things that we need protection and freedom from. We need to put distance between us and the things to which we've become bound.

Paul told Timothy to instruct those who had become their own enemy (2 Timothy 2:24). This was so they would repent and turn to God and recover themselves. The Lord truly wants to grant them repentance so that they will know the truth (2 Timothy 2:25).

Believers in Jesus Christ can become their own worst enemies when they wrestle against themselves. They love the Lord, but can't seem to conquer a certain stronghold of the enemy in their life. God will certainly grant them deliverance, through repentance, by acknowledging the truth. This is true, even if facing that truth may be painful.

When ministering to fellow believers, you will hear them speak of things that have become enemies to them. Through this, you will begin to see where they're opposing themselves by things they do not perceive. Ask the Holy Spirit to lead and guide you by His wisdom as you minister to them. Be gentle and patient. They will eventually begin to see what they couldn't perceive before, as the Word of God (the truth) is presented to the area where they are in bondage. When they come into agreement with the Word of God, they progressively recover themselves, and are released from the snare of the devil (2 Timothy 2:26).

When does bondage take hold in life?

Childhood is the most vulnerable time in every person's life. It's where bondage can take root. A little child cannot understand or describe his own personality, so life's circumstances tend to dictate the shape they take. It's easy to receive things in childhood that establish the way you are. It is a time of great vulnerability. A whole set of self-rejection patterns begin in early childhood; especially if there isn't proper love, affection, acceptance, and value attributed to that precious little one.

Another area where bondage may set in is during puberty. Children are extremely vulnerable to change. This is a perfect time for the enemy to ensnare some sharp hooks into the soul and manipulate children to become as difficult as they can be. Rebellion, depression, and confusion can set in at this time. This is also when youthful points of control and bondage in a young person's life are established by the wicked one.

Pregnancy is also another critical time where bondage can take place. There are great waves of emotions and physical challenges as a woman's body is changing. They become vulnerable in that season of life as chemical changes are happening in their bodies. They're not sure how to respond to all of these changes, so bondage may very well occur at this point.

<u>Other occasions when bondage can take hold</u>

Other times when bondage may take hold are during menopause or mid-life crisis, an accident or tragedy, or maybe with an unwed mother giving up her baby for adoption, or a person raised as an only child, the influence of foster parents (those only doing it for the money), a divorce, a split-home (where only one parent is saved), orphaned because of the death of a parent, and when the father is absent. None of these things have to dictate bondage, but they sometimes provide the climate and occasion for it.

Then, there is the case of an absent father (I personally experienced this in a profound way). There's a profound impact and deficiency in the lives of those whose father was gone. The father may be gone on business a lot, away because of illness, or abandonment...emotionally unavailable for the child. This creates deep insecurity in many people. This insecurity creates places for long-term spiritual bondage in a person's life. I know about this one firsthand, because my own father up and left my mother and me when I was nine years-old. This brought great pain and what felt like unshakable chains of bondage to drugs, alcohol, and immorality upon my soul (mind, will, and emotions) that wasn't broken until well into my adult years.

Others experience tension, rancor and upheaval in the home. A person may also enter an area of bondage because they can never please their parent. Having never received the approval they needed, the enemy enters in at that point. There's also the social setting of a person's home that can lead a person into bondage. If there's continual poverty or immorality there, this kind of atmosphere can open a door and invite Satan's control into a person's life.

The main objective in this chapter is to define areas where bondage potentially takes root in a person's life. As we draw near to the truth of the Word of God and come into agreement with it, we can repent and experience the freedom God has always intended for us to have. If we determine the point where the enemy entered and established control, we can expel these youthful lusts in the mighty Name of

Jesus and by the power of His blood. There is freedom for you from these points of control and the enemy's chains of bondage!

Deliverance from sin

Knowing this, that our old man was crucified with Him, that the body of sin might be done away with, that we should no longer be slaves of sin. For he who has died has been freed from sin. Now if we died with Christ, we believe that we shall also live with Him, knowing that Christ, having been raised from the dead, dies no more. Death no longer has dominion over Him. For the death that He died, He died to sin once for all; but the life that He lives, He lives to God. Likewise, you also, reckon yourselves to be dead indeed to sin, but alive to God in Christ Jesus our Lord.

Therefore, do not let sin reign in your mortal body, that you should obey it in its lusts. And do not present your members as instruments of righteousness to God. For sin shall not have dominion over you, for you are not under law but under grace.

What then? Shall we sin because we are not under law but under grace? Certainly not! Do you not know that to whom you present yourselves slaves to obey, you are that one's slaves whom you obey, whether of sin leading to death, or of obedience leading to righteousness? But God be thanked that though you were slaves of sin, yet you obeyed from the heart that form of doctrine to which you were delivered. And having been set free from sin, you became slaves of righteousness. I speak in human terms because of the weakness of your flesh. For just as you presented your members as slaves of uncleanness, and of lawlessness leading to more lawlessness, so now present your members as slaves of righteousness for holiness.

For when you were slaves of sin, you were free in regard to righteousness. What fruit did you have then in the things of which you are now ashamed? For the end of those things is death. But now having been set free from sin, and having become slaves of God, you have your fruit to holiness, and the end, everlasting life. For the wages of sin is death, but the gift of God is eternal life in Christ Jesus our Lord. (Romans 6:6-23)

For when you were slaves of sin, you were free in regard to righteousness. What fruit did you have then in the things of which you are now ashamed? For the end of those things is death. But now having been set free from sin, and having become slaves of God, you have your fruit to holiness, and the end, everlasting life. For the wages of sin is death, but the gift of God is eternal life in Christ Jesus our Lord.

Deliverance is an integral part of the message the Lord gave to His Church.

"The Spirit of the Lord God is upon Me, Because the Lord has anointed Me to preach good tidings to the poor; He has sent Me to heal the brokenhearted, to proclaim liberty to the captives, and the opening of the prison to those who are bound." (Isaiah 61:1)

Deliverance is the only aspect of ministry to which the Lord had to caution His disciples.

Then the seventy returned with joy, saying, "Lord, even the demons are subject to us in Your Name." And He said to them, "I saw Satan fall like lightning from heaven. Behold, I give you the authority to trample on serpents and scorpions, and over all the power of the enemy, and nothing shall by any means hurt you. Nevertheless, do not rejoice in this, that the spirits are subject to you, but rather rejoice because your names are written in heaven." (Luke 10:17-20)

Notice Jesus didn't say, "Don't do it." He told them to keep their perspective. Today, we are still very much like the early disciples. People will rise to shout and rejoice far more readily if someone tells about a miraculous healing than if they testify they led their friend to the Lord. Often the subject of deliverance is taught as it pertains to the casting out of satanic power.

"And these signs will follow those who believe: In My Name they will cast out demons; they will speak with new tongues; they will take up serpents; and if they drink anything deadly, it will by no means hurt them; they will lay hands on the sick, and they will recover." (Mark 16:17-18)

This authority is given to believers in the Name of Jesus Christ as they move in the power of God's Kingdom. It is vital, however, to keep in mind that deliverance is about the whole process of salvation.

The reality is that deliverance is a past, present and future matter! As the Bible says, God has made us to sit in heavenly places in Christ. As we sit with Him, all powers are brought beneath our feet! Again, deliverance is a past, present and future matter.

"Who delivered us from so great a death, and does deliver us; in Whom we trust that He will still deliver us." (2 Corinthians 1:10)

Sin is the reason we need deliverance. The present, ongoing delivering process of the Lord Jesus, according to the Bible, is from the works of the flesh (self), and the works of Satan. With regard to the future, the Bible speaks of a day of ultimate deliverance from this decaying body into our eternal, glorified body to be with God (1 Corinthians 15; 1 Thessalonians 4).

<u>Regarding our past: deliverance from the penalty of sin</u>

The wages of sin are death (Romans 6:23); thus, this is the penalty of sin. Sin pays off. Because all have sinned and come short of the glory of

God, there is no possibility, no hope for human flesh outside of a man Named Jesus of Nazareth, Who came to save us from our sins (Matthew 1:18). The name "Jesus" in the Old Testament is "Joshua." It means "Savior" or "Deliverer." The whole message of the cross of Christ is deliverance: that we're delivered from the penalty of sin, sickness, demons, and fear.

Regarding the present: manifestations of sin

These manifestations of sin are:

- The works of the flesh;
- The works of Satan; and
- sickness.

Satan does attack believers to be sure, but know that an attack is not at all the same as bondage. Sometimes a person is simply facing the temptations that come to all of us. There often seems to be a great problem discerning between self and Satan. One mode of teaching says it's a matter of victory over self (in other words, you just need discipline). Another mode attributes absolutely everything to satanic attack (meaning that you need deliverance). Each is probably the case about fifty percent of the time. The purpose of discernment between self and the devil is so you can face your adversary—be it self or the devil—and conquer.

First, sin finds its method of operation in our greatest enemy—self. Obviously, you cannot cast out 'self.' What you can do is obey God's Word and:

- Reckon yourself dead unto sin but alive unto God (Romans 6:11);
- Put to death [mortify] your members which are upon the earth (Colossians 3:5);
- Be crucified with Christ. (Galatians 2:20)

Second, we have a great adversary in Satan. who agitated and stimulated the rebellion in man. He fans the possibilities of sin in us daily. Satan will often find a place to set up camp among the clinging vines of the fall in our human nature. If a believer can be filled with the Holy Spirit and moved by the Lord, Satan can find a means of expression to assault your nature, even though you truly love the Lord. Peter is an example of a disciple susceptible to the wiles and manifestations of the enemy.

Simon Peter answered and said, "You are the Christ, the Son of the living God."

Jesus answered and said to him, "Blessed are you, Simon Bar-Jonah, for flesh and blood has not revealed this to you, but My Father Who is in heaven. And I also say to you that you are Peter, and on this rock I will build My church, and the gates of Hades shall not prevail against it. And I will give you the keys of the kingdom of heaven, and whatever you bind on earth will be bound in heaven, and whatever you loose on earth will be loosed in heaven."

Then He commanded His disciples that they should tell no one that He was Jesus the Christ. From that time Jesus began to show to His disciples that He must go to Jerusalem, and suffer many things from the elders and chief priests and scribes, and be killed, and be raised the third day.

Then Peter took Him aside and began to rebuke Him, saying, "Far be it from You, Lord; this shall not happen to You!"

But He turned and said to Peter, "Get behind Me, Satan! You are an offense to Me, for you are not mindful of the things of God, but the things of men." (Matthew 16:16-23)

The third manifestation of sin is sickness and disease. These are the great enemies of the human race. Jesus did not say to cast out sickness. There is a place for healing the sick and casting out demons (Matthew 10:1). Some sickness literally is the manifestation of demonic presence, and that spirit(s) needs to be cast out if healing is going to be possible, but that's not every case. These are the means by which sin finds the possibility of manifesting itself and Jesus has a way He's given to the Church to deal with each of them. In every case, you can call this deliverance.

Where we find deliverance from sin

Deliverance from sin comes from the acceptance and obedience to the authority of Christ. It would be easy if we could just cast out our selfish tendencies, but that's not how this works. The only way to be free of the sin of self is to grow by feeding on the Word, speaking it with power and authority, and walking in obedience. God desires to develop the image and character of Jesus in each of us. We are to contend in all three of the following areas of proclaiming deliverance to the captive:

- Deliverance from the penalty of sin is acceptance of the grace of God through Jesus Christ and His finished work. It's our privilege and responsibility to go to people, put loving arm around them and say, "Hey, Jesus loves you, and He really will forgive your sins." The Holy Spirit will enable you to show the love of Jesus, and people will sense that it is genuine, and there surely is freedom from their sins in it.

- Deliverance from immaturity comes through obedience to the Word of God and the conquering of self through acknowledging the truth and the way of righteousness is through Jesus alone. His life in you is key to triumph and you can stand in the power of His life.

- Deliverance from the slavery of sin comes through the delegated authority granted to all believers in Jesus Christ and our faith in His finished work at the Cross to take dominion wherever that slavery is discovered to be still present.

When we truly trust and obey, there is a pathway of joy in our walk with Jesus that continues to expand and open up to us. We need to grow in discernment and also lovingly confront people with the truth:

- In the compassion of Jesus Christ and the gentleness of the Lord;
- With wisdom that surpasses Solomon's, coming only from Jesus;
- To deal with them in the authority of the message of the cross;
- To cast out demons and see people stand in the freedom of the Lord;
- Then to take them with the same arms of love and compassion and open to them the Word of God, and
- Teaching them how they can conquer sin through faith in the finished work of the cross, so they don't open up to it again.

CHAPTER THREE

DELIVERANCE FOR THE WHOLE PERSON

**NOW MAY THE GOD OF PEACE
HIMSELF SANCTIFY YOU COMPLETELY;
AND MAY YOUR WHOLE SPIRIT, SOUL,
AND BODY BE PRESERVED BLAMELESS
AT THE COMING OF OUR LORD JESUS CHRIST. HE
WHO CALLS YOU IS FAITHFUL,
WHO ALSO WILL DO IT.
(1 THESSALONIANS 5:23-24)**

Victory

The Kingdom of God enters into any specific area of our lives where the Lord desires victory or deliverance with power. The Spirit of God places His finger at the point where He wants to heal and set us free, then casts out demons and overcomes their hellish activities. Varying degrees of dominion can oppress or enslave a human being, although once again, a believer cannot be possessed. When a person does not have the indwelling of the Holy Spirit nor the insulating protection of the Spirit of God in their lives, that individual can be "demonized" by the works of hell. They do not have the resources of the living God and His Son, the Lord Jesus Christ ruling and reigning inside of them.

When we expose ourselves to something sinful (by our own will or ignorance), by reason of things transmitted to us through generations, or things that are done or allowed, we became exposed and vulnerable to demonic activity in our lives. The allegiance of these demonic hordes is to Satan. They move under his direction, serving his purposes as he seeks to steal, kill and destroy human beings. Even when you and I become born again, we still remain in the arena where spiritual conflict, attack and oppression take place. No matter what degree of victory we find through Jesus Christ, we will find He has another stage of victory awaiting us. There is something inherent in the word "victory" that means there is no such thing unless there is first a battle. There are no testimonies without great tests. Great faith will be tested greatly.

God's view of humanity

We live in a lost and unbelieving world that generally regards man as having two natures: emotional and intellectual. God views every one of us as a tripartite being (having a spirit, soul and body). Just as there are three parts to our human nature, there are three parts to God's nature: Father, Son and Holy Spirit. Your spirit being is the real you. The spirit is our God-consciousness. When we become born again, our human spirit is ignited by the light of the Lord (Proverbs 20:27; John 1:9) and God writes the witness of Himself upon our heart; in other words, He brings a revelation of who He is (Romans 1:19-21). Paul says we are born as creatures inclined to sin (Romans 7:9). This is because we are all wired for sin from birth, and this comes from our fallen nature (those clinging vines of the fall). Before Christ's saving grace, we were manipulated by, rebelled and walked in the spirit of this world. There was no internal force of the life of God in us to resist anything other than simply responding to whatever were the impulses and directives of the world. We were blind to sin (Ephesians 2:1-5: 2 Corinthians 4:4). When we are saved, we are alive in Christ and die to sin. The sin nature becomes dormant...the plug is pulled.

The soul is our self-consciousness. The soul consists of the mind, will, and emotions. The command center of our human personality is our soul. The Bible draws a clear line between the soul and the spirit, but our culture lumps them both together. They do this because there is not a relatedness to God, His Spirit, His rule, His power, or His life. When we talk about emotion or the intellect, we are basically talking about those influences that govern my actions. The will is the interaction of these two parts of me—they converge and move me towards decisions which I make on the basis of my will. The emotion and the intellect become basic points of vicious attacks by the evil one.

Satan distorts, twists and turns our feelings and minds because he wants us to make decisions that are outside of the will of God. He tempts and manipulate us to reason and rationalize our own way and to feel differently than we should.

Satan also uses pride, which is the common and root problem with mankind. Pride is actually a manifestation of fear; it's what we do to prove that we are not afraid. It's an attempt to cover it all up.

The enemy attacks us in the areas of doubt, unbelief and fear. Almost everything we deal with in the human personality that steals one's peace will one way or the other come under the category of these two things: regeneration and rebirth.

Regeneration and rebirth

We escape darkness and spiritual bondage by coming into the light of Jesus Christ. When God's word enters us, we decide whether to receive it or not. When we are born again, we are reborn from death to life, from darkness to light and from blindness to sight. The inner man is restored by a well of water springing up, which brings eternal life and opens us to the flow and fullness of the Holy Spirit. John 7:37-39 tells us that out of our hearts will flow living water when we believe in Jesus. Here is a simple comparison: salvation is like a well - it contains life giving water which satisfies our thirst and helps us to survive. The Baptism with the Holy Spirit is like a river that flows through us and overflows, bringing life to all.

Attacks and cheap shots from the enemy

There are lots of ways the enemy attacks our body, through various afflictions or influencing our mind and emotions. He masterminds and plots from the pit, and wants to take control the universe and those who are in it. When we come to Christ, Satan will inevitably attack us to retain whatever control he can. Sometimes his attacks make it past the chinks in our armor through special circumstances such as:

- Times of tragedy and/or bondage (severing points, such as divorce, death of a family member or through accidents or disasters)
- Times of great disappointment
- Times of emotional or physiological upheaval and transition (such as childhood, puberty, pregnancy and menopause, effectng both men and women)
- Acts of outright disobedience as well as through exposure to or playing around with the occult

Fending off attacks and cheap shots from the enemy

When we are armed with the supernatural provisions and weapons that God supplies, we are then prepared for spiritual warfare (Ephesians 6). Something sets us up in the atmosphere that consumes those things which bombard us. Lamentations 3:22 says that because of the mercies of the Lord we are not consumed, because His compassions never fail. The grace of God will always hinder the hateful onslaughts of hell.

Putting our complete faith in the finished work of Christ on the cross opens us up to the flow of the Holy Spirit. This allows Him to deliver us from bitterness or unforgiveness; from any habits or behaviors which cause us to come under the influence of controlling things. In order to walk in this victory the cross freely gives, we must determine not to give place to the devil and exhibit willingness to be delivered and freed from the things which hinder or sever our relationship with God.

Deliverance from sickness and disease

"If you diligently heed the voice of the Lord your God and do what is right in His sight, give ear to His commandments and keep all His statutes, I will put none of the diseases on you which I have brought on the Egyptians. For I am the Lord Who heals you." (Exodus 15:26)

This text refers to the covenant God made with His chosen people, sealing it by revealing Himself as the Lord Who heals. The people are told that if they will walk in a covenant relationship with Him, the Lord will release them from His hand of judgment. Seven times in the Old Testament, God reveals Himself to His people by one of what are called the compound names of Jehovah. This one is "'Jehovah-Rophe,' the Lord who is healing you." He is revealed as the eternal, unchanging Lord who declares He will constantly be available to heal for all time.

The Old Covenant of healing

In the most widely known prophecy of the Old Testament, Isaiah 53:3-12 vividly shows that the Messiah would suffer and die in our place.

He is despised and rejected by men, a Man of sorrows and acquainted with grief. And we hid, as it were, our faces from Him; He was despised, and we did not esteem Him.

Surely He has borne our griefs and carried our sorrows; yet we esteemed Him stricken, Smitten by God, and afflicted. But He was wounded for our transgressions, He was bruised for our iniquities; the chastisement for our peace was upon Him, and by His stripes we are healed. All we like sheep have gone astray; we have turned, every one, to his own way; and the LORD has laid on Him the iniquity of us all.

He was oppressed and He was afflicted, yet He opened not His mouth; He was led as a lamb to the slaughter, and as a sheep before its shearers is silent, so He opened not His mouth. He was taken from prison and from judgment, and who will declare His generation? For He was cut off from the land of the living; for the transgressions of My people He was stricken. And they made His grave with the wicked—But with the rich at His death, Because He had done no violence, Nor was any deceit in His mouth.

Yet it pleased the LORD to bruise Him; He has put Him to grief. When You make His soul an offering for sin, He shall see His seed, He shall prolong His days, And the pleasure of the LORD shall prosper in His hand. He shall see the labor of His soul, and be satisfied. By His knowledge My righteous Servant shall justify many, For He shall bear their iniquities.

Therefore I will divide Him a portion with the great, and He shall divide the spoil with the *strong, because He poured out His soul unto death, and He was numbered with the transgressors, and He bore the sin of many, and made intercession for the transgressors.*

While the shedding of His blood on the cross was essential to the washing away of our sins, and as He endured separation from the Father for the weight of our guilt upon Him, the physical pain and anguish Jesus suffered on the Cross was not just for the cleansing of sins, but for the provision that people may be healed of sickness and delivered from disease. At Calvary, atonement was made for the restoration of man spiritually, mentally, emotionally and physically.

The New Covenant of healing

The ministry of divine healing is not an option or some tiny footnote hanging on the side of the Gospel. It is wrapped up in the very heart of the total provision of God for us in Christ. God created us: spirit, soul and body. He is interested in our redemption and deliverance in every aspect of life. The good news is that at the cross, there is full deliverance in every dimension of man and woman's being, including healing.

The Old Covenant is fulfilled in the New Covenant

The New Testament application of Isaiah 53:4 is revealed in Matthew 8:16-17, and directly related to an instance where Jesus is healing all who come to Him. In John 14:12, Jesus says that we will do the things He does and greater, and Jesus healed all.

Why can't we heal all?

There may not be a satisfactory answer for this question. Regardless, may the church rise in the authority and the power of His Name as the body of Christ to welcome all, to pray for all, and to minister to all. In Matthew 28:18, Jesus said:

"All power is given to Me in heaven and in earth."

Jesus Christ has ordained a means by which His Church may be sustained in health. The sick among us are told to call upon the elders for prayer (James 5:14).

God has committed Himself to you by a revelation of Himself in a Name. In the Old Testament covenant, He said, "I am Jehovah Rophe; I am the Lord, your healer." In the New Testament, He has revealed Himself to us fully: His Name is Jesus and He shall deliver His people from all their sins and everything related to them.

Strangely enough, when I preach or teach on the subject of divine healing, I often get attacked with sickness or confronted with some great challenge. It doesn't take a lot of discernment to figure out the source of it. If this great Bible truth was not worth preaching and teaching, then Satan wouldn't contend against it.

Confronting evil with fervent, Spirit-empowered prayer

(See 1 Kings, chapter 18)

Here we will examine how the principles contained here in this Old Testament passage are New Testament principles. Verse 1 gives us a basic outline of what we're going to talk about. The balance of the chapter tells how the instruction the Lord gave Elijah was lived out. These principles are applicable to our lives.

Fervent prayer

James 5:16-18 tells us:

Confess your trespasses to one another, and pray for one another, that you may be healed. The effective, fervent prayer of a righteous man avails much. Elijah was a man with a nature like ours, and he prayed earnestly that it would not rain; and it did not rain on the land for three years and six months. And he prayed again, and the heaven gave rain, and the earth produced its fruit.

The effectual fervent prayer of a righteous man avails much. This means it is prayer that turns things around, a prayer of faith that gets results, changes circumstances, and is powerful. We see Elijah praying fervently, with the energy that the Holy Spirit gives. He prayed in a fashion to release transformation to his circumstance. The blessing of God released into that circumstance where it had not been moving before.

Evil rule

The Lord sent Elijah to King Ahab after three-and-a-half years of no rain. Ahab's wife Jezebel was from Canaan (he went and brought her to Israel for that very reason), worshipped Ba'al, and had many prophets killed. Yes, Ahab was an evil king. We recognize the root of that evil is Satan, because Satan is the king of evil.

When the Old Testament speaks of idolatry, it's not just talking about liking a celebrity or following someone closely on social media. Old Testament examples of idolatry revolved around religious groups that were totally devoted to false gods and goddesses. Ba'al and Ashtoreth were two such deities. Ba'al worship and Ashtoreth worship were related, as Ba'al was considered the "lord" of Ashtoreth. As a fertility cult, their worship involved elaborate rites of sex magic. Anyone and anything would engage in diverse sexual activities (as part of their "spells") for the purpose of inspiring procreation, successful crops, animal husbandry, and prosperity.

The worship of Ba'al and Ashtoreth were, at their base, the worship of perverted sex. What God ordained to be a pure, powerful, and fulfilling part of human experience was perverted and debased in every possible form.

The confrontation

Elijah going before Ahab face-to-face is a case of a prophet of God confronting a person who rules in the evil realm. The objective was to release the rain of blessing that God intended to rain down on the people. Elijah challenged the prophets of Ba'al to have their gods answer by fire, but they did not. Elijah repaired the altar of the Lord, called upon Him, and the fire of God fell and consumed everything. All the people said, "The Lord, He is God!"

Elijah built the altar, called upon the Name of the Lord, put the wood in order, and cut the bullock in pieces. Elijah knew he had no grounds to confront evil and advance the claims of God apart from offering a sacrifice, according to God's order.

There's no victory accomplished unless we point back to draw on the resource of the sacrifice. By a specific point of understanding, in this battle, you have to see the intensity of the conflict. You have to see the bleeding and battered body of Jesus on the cross and listen to Him saying all power is given to Him, and for us to go and extend that. God has called us to build an altar where we learn to enter into confrontational prayer; to see hell broken down in its workings. These are times where fervency, the Holy Spirit energized prayer of a redeemed righteous person counts for a whole lot; travailing prayer, and spiritual warfare.

After the fire fell, Elijah had the people seize the prophets of Ba'al and execute them, right then and there. The Lord is not interested in just demonstrating His power; He wants there to be a total release of His blessing in that situation. Elijah went to the top of Carmel and began to pray, because the rain hadn't come. With his face to the ground between his knees, he began to travail until he saw the re-instating of God's order of things. Then, the rain began pouring down!

The pattern: We must cast away tameness, timidity and passivity, and begin to seek God, understanding it is not our energy or our zeal that gets God to do anything. Instead, it's an evidence of our participation, here on earth, as we understand we're not dealing with small matters or issues. We are dealing with great issues that should occupy our emotions and passions as we are stirred up and begin to seek the Lord and to come against the powers of darkness. As we do this, we'll see the confrontation of evil and the power of fervently seeking after God: evil is broken and God's blessing falls on situations, and fruitfulness begins to come after long dry spells.

James chapter 5 teaches that the energized prayer of a righteous person avails much; so, we pray and seek hard after Him. Every one of us should have built up an altar where we can go, as needed, to seek hard after God for breakthrough and turning around the forces of evil.

Deliverance from self

What shall we say then? Shall we continue in sin that grace may abound? Certainly not! How shall we who died to sin live any longer in it? Or do you not know that as many of us were baptized into Christ Jesus were baptized into His death? Therefore, we were buried with Him through baptism into death, that just as Christ was raised from the dead by the glory of the Father, even so we also should walk in newness of life.

For if we have been united together in the likeness of His death, certainly we also shall be in the likeness of His resurrection, knowing this, that our old man was crucified with Him, that the body of sin might be done away with, that we should no longer be slaves of sin. For he who has died has been freed from sin. Now if we died with Christ, we believe that we shall also live with Him, knowing that Christ, having been raised from the dead, dies no more. Death no longer has dominion over Him. For the death that He died, He died to sin once for all; but the life that He lives, He lives to God. Likewise, you also, reckon yourselves to be dead indeed to sin, but alive to God in Christ Jesus our Lord.

Therefore, do not let sin reign in your mortal body, that you should obey it in its lusts. And do not present your members as instruments of unrighteousness to sin, but present yourselves to God as being alive from the dead, and your members as instruments of righteousness to God. For sin shall not have dominion over you, for you are not under law but under grace.
(Romans 6:1-14)

People want to be free. The many modern liberation movements prove that people seek deliverance and freedom. However, outside of coming to the Lord Jesus Christ (Isaiah 61:1-11), people tend to trade off one form of bondage for another and call it "freedom." The most obvious form of humankind's bondage is to sin. Without Jesus Christ, a person is bound in chains of spiritual death (Ephesians 2:1). We are not talking about sin as a principle or an act, but as a power that controls a person who is outside of Jesus Christ. For the believer, even though there may be sporadic attempts of sin that crop up in the flesh, sin is no longer a continuous way of life (He that is born of God does not keep on sinning, 1 John 3:9). The Lord Jesus, by setting us free from bondage to spiritual death, has established a pattern by which He sets us free at every dimension of our being.

Deliverance from the devil and deliverance from self

Probably the greatest enemy that the average believer has isn't so much our adversary the devil, as it is my adversary, ME— my ego, my will, and my pride. Deliverance from self does not happen in one glorious instant, like deliverance from demonic oppression. It takes place when we enter a pattern of walking by faith in Jesus Christ and Him crucified: discovering truth in the Word, and abiding in that confession. Deliverance from self requires self-discipline and a continuing faith in the finished work of the cross rather than a moment of delivering faith that comes upon you.

Dead to sin

Romans chapters 4 and 5 outline the principle that we are justified by faith (Romans 5:1). You can be comfortable in the Lord's presence, because of the confidence that your soul has been established in righteousness before God. On that basis, Paul begins Chapter 6, verse 1 by saying,

"Since God has so lavished His forgiving grace upon us, that He declares us— regardless of our weakness and sinfulness—to be holy in His sight, shall we just then go on sinning so that God can keep showing His grace? God forbid."

The literal Greek expression in this verse is, "Let it never be so!" Here, he introduces a new concept: you are dead to sin. When you were baptized in Christ (verse 3), you entered (by faith) into His full provision. Among other benefits, this causes you to stand perfect in the sight of God. Jesus died for all sin and sinning; not just for all sins committed to that point in time, but for all sins ever to be committed. We're talking sins past, present, and future! Jesus died to everything that makes sin arise, and that has to do with our nature and tendency to sin.

The law of sin and death

There is a law, a principle of sin (Romans 7) true of the person who is double-mindedly tossed back and forth by their own nature—the flesh—warring for its place in their life. Paul is talking about somebody who delights in the law of God, but sees another law warring in his mind and bringing him to captivity (Romans 7:23). This is someone who wants to do right and then doesn't do it. Paul says, "The Lord has brought me alive in Jesus, and I'm dragging this dead man around. How in heaven's name can I get rid of it?" The answer is in the ministry of the Holy Spirit, which teaches us how to triumph over ourselves as well as over the wicked one.

The triumphant ministry of the Holy Spirit

Much like the law of gravity that drags a person down (no matter how much you might try to argue with it), the Apostle Paul says there is a law of sin in my flesh that drags me down. It's not the devil; it's me. Yet now I see another law – the law of the Spirit of life in Christ Jesus which has made me free from the law of sin and death (Romans 8:2). That airplane will stay earth-bound forever on its own. If you put fuel in it, it will do what it was made to do. The law of the Holy Spirit gives us adequate power to live free of the law of sin. The ministry of the Holy Spirit is given to you and me:

- To enter into an area of discerning spiritual warfare;
- To increase our love for God's Word;
- To increase our desire to worship Jesus;
- For the privilege of a new level of communication with the Father through our supernatural utterance;

- To witness to the unsaved; and
- More importantly, to teach us the pathway of deliverance from ourselves.

Our old man is put out of business

To live in the likeness of His resurrection (verse 5) means that our "our old man"—our self-life—is crucified with Christ, that the body of sin might be put out of business (so it isn't in control anymore). You can put yourself down every day and have the enemy right alongside you, encouraging you to do so. Satan is working hand-in-hand with our flesh or self-life. When he can't get a place of dominion in the personality, he'll do everything he can to foster your dominion. While you're there saying, "I don't want to," you still find something cropping up inside. How do you deal with that?

Count on your being dead to sin

The word "reckon" was used in ancient bookkeeping practices, and as it is used here in Romans 6:11, it means "You can count on it because it is completely accurate. It is the sum of truth. If you put the pieces together, that's exactly how it comes out." You can count on it. Paul is saying to count on this: you are indeed dead to sin. It's not just a way of "thinking," it's a way of "reckoning." Trust the One Who did something on the cross of Calvary not only to forgive you of your sins, but to make you triumphant over self and the sin principle that works in you.

It works by faith. You can now choose as to whether you will move in that direction with confidence, joy and assurance, or grumbling and griping at yourself all the way as to why you haven't arrived yet. The Lord is going to see that you get there. As long as you keep on letting Jesus work His love and His goodness in your life, you're going to arrive at His grand purpose for you. You can complain and condemn yourself, or you can decide what He said about you is true. Because of your faith in the cross of Christ, God has declared you justified in His sight, so the Father declares you holy. In the meantime, the Lord says to regard yourself dead to sin. No, you may not be the model of perfection, but when you finally accept who you are by the Word of God in Christ Jesus, you'll have a degree of confidence and ability to function as an overcomer.

Romans 7:24 says:

"Who shall deliver me from this body of death?"

The deeper perspective of this passage is found in a little history about Roman punishments. The Romans would punish murderers by having them carry the corpse of their victim, bound and attached to their own back, so tightly as to not be able to extricate themselves from it. In time, the weight, shame, mental torment, and stench of it would be too much to bear; not to mention the fact that sickness and disease would eventually overcome the convicted killer, with the rotting carcass (body of death) being the death of him. That is what unconfessed sin does to the soul and spirit of a human being.

As horrible as this sounds, please read on, because there is Good News for you and me, as well as for the entire human race!

CHAPTER FOUR

STREAMS OF DELIVERANCE

BUT IN A GREAT HOUSE THERE ARE NOT ONLY VESSELS OF GOLD AND SILVER, BUT ALSO OF WOOD AND CLAY, SOME FOR HONOR AND SOME FOR DISHONOR.
(2 TIMOTHY 2:20)

Designed to be vessels of honor

In this chapter, we will look at the bondages that hinder us from becoming vessels of honor and how to gain our freedom. Paul uses household vessels as an analogy of us before God. There are vessels of honor, and vessels of dishonor. He urges young Timothy to purge himself from everything that would hinder him from being a vessel of honor for God. What type of vessel that you and I are depends on our choices. We are each given the responsibility to allow the Holy Spirit to purge us with His holy fire. We are to be a vessel full of the light and life of our God.

In and of ourselves, we're unable to determine where the body stops and the soul begins. Demonic powers, however, can attach themselves to us like leeches. They will suck the life out of us and drain us of our life force if we let them. We are instructed by God to put off the old flesh (self) – the way of the world – and be renewed in the spirit of our minds.

You put off, concerning your former conduct, the old man which grows corrupt according to the deceitful lusts, and be renewed in the spirit of your mind, and that you put on the new man which was created according to God, in true righteousness and holiness. (Ephesians 4:22-24)

The wicked one attaches himself to us through our thoughts and feelings when we repeatedly give place to him. An example of this is by allowing depression to hang over you, rather than putting on the garment of praise. If you allow something to become a way of life, it will become a dominant trait.

As a blood-bought, born again child of God, you cannot be possessed by a demon, because the Holy Spirit possesses you (1 John 4:3). Satan will attempt to bring hell to and upon us. His attacks are like meteors in the atmosphere; most of them are consumed before they hit the earth. Most attacks from the adversary are consumed by the covering presence of God (Ephesians 6). However, if we are not walking in the Spirit, but rather giving place for the lust of the flesh, these attacks will successfully penetrate our soul.

Many bondages enter into our lives through

past experiences that occur in our development years (2 Timothy 2:22). The enemy convinces us to use these experiences as an excuse for bad or unhealthy behavior. Some of these entry points are:

- Lack of self-discipline
- Disappointments
- The failure of an authority figure
- Sexual violation
- Times of physical change like puberty, pregnancy or menopause
- Negative peer pressure
- Accidents and their aftermath
- Traumatic times or war; i.e. PTSD

There are four types of bondage that we can identify in the Word of God.

- Sin – Who and what we were in before we met Jesus
- Sickness – Affliction
- Self – The flesh (we have the capacity to sin without any satanic help)
- Satan – Many believers become frustrated because they have done all that they know to do to be free, and yet

they aren't. At this point, they need a spirit cast out of them. This does not mean they are demon-possessed, but there is an evil spirit in control.

The Apostle Paul invites us to become a vessel of honor by purging ourselves of everything that hinders us from being this vessel. Our spiritual growth requires repentance; which is a constant willingness on our part to accept discipline. Truth and love are two agents producing liberty in our lives (John 8:32; Romans 5:5). The flow of the Word of God (truth) will loosen the hold of the enemy. The Holy Spirit (God's love shed abroad in our hearts) produces a flood that uproots bondage. We are to get into God's word and pray in the Holy Spirit and let the river of deliverance rise and flush the dishonorable things away.

We are vessels of deliverance

(Reading: Exodus chapters 3 and 4)

The Lord is calling us up to a higher place in Him. Here, we learn more of His nature and ways; becoming people who go past just viewing His acts to people who are learning His ways of operation. As we move into that greater grasp of Himself and greater openness to His person, there comes the qualification for deliverance.

- **The Lord calls Moses as His instrument of deliverance for the chosen people** – Three things qualify him for this. The Lord: (1) tells Moses He is going to make him the person who will cause other people's release; (2) shows Himself to Moses in a way he didn't understand before to make it possible for him to minister more of God; and (3) confirms Moses' words with signs following.

- **What the Lord is doing today** – He is revealing more of Himself, shedding greater light on His own person, through His Word, than at any time in church history. The church is moving into conflict with dark powers, into battles en masse, when it has not previously. He is calling the Church at large into a place of ministry, into an availability of His workings, into sharing with Him in travail that will birth another age.

- **The Lord deals with Moses' relationships** – God dealt with Moses from the time He called him to be an instrument of deliverance until he became that instrument (Exodus 4:18-31). God doesn't allow Moses to arrive to that place of ministry He prophesied until each one of these matters is settled correctly. The three levels are how we relate to: (1) authority over us; (2) those people under us; and (3) those who are with us (peers).

- **The Lord prepares Moses** – Jethro holds three offices in reference to Moses – (1) employer (economic), (2) father-in-law (domestic), and (3) spiritual leadership (authority). Jethro was the High Priest of Midian. Moses asked "Will you let me go?" He rests the fulfillment of a ministry God called him to upon the whim of the answer of a man who had authority over him. He doesn't try to pressure Jethro, but he operates under phenomenal grace. Moses' approach to Jethro was in a faith that respects God's order in a paternal relationship and in a faith that makes inquiry and refuses to make demands.

- **The Lord calls the church** – The church has received a revelation similar to that of Moses. As Moses went into Egypt to deliver Israel, the church enters into a deliverance of nations. God wants to make a Moses out of every one of us – an instrument of deliverance of a nation.

- **There are still hindrances to overcome** – The Lord wants to bring an awareness to the Church that He will do things in the life of the body of Christ today that will upset the status quo, but things happen to hinder that:

- **Internal relationships** – Satan strikes at the key place of crippling the church: internal relationships. This effectively cripples the Church for battle. No army can assail its adversaries successfully with broken ranks. Submission has to do with correct positioning, with accepting the place you've been assigned. When we don't receive the place He gives us, it doesn't release the ministry He gives us. The purpose of submission is for the release of authority.

- **Seeking someone else's authority** – Authority is defined as being what you've been created to be in the power you've been given to be that. True authority is the unfolding and releasing of what I was created to be. God is dishonored when we try to force any one of us into the mold of how somebody else has been called to be. We hinder His work through us.

- **An unforgiving spirit** – This is a major hindrance that binds up what could happen through a fellow servant. I wonder how many have been trapped and stymied in the possibility of their movement into an enlarged revelation of God's purposes in this day by a hard, unforgiving attitude, a kind of spiritual snobbery that prevails in subtle, refined manifestations in other members of the body of Christ.

Instruments of deliverance are brought out of right relationships. Philippians 2:3 tells us to "esteem others better than ourselves." Submitting to one another is to acknowledge those who are our peers as being over us or above us in some way in the things of God. Here, we can operate under the same grace Moses did with Jethro: through submission and trust. It begins by recognizing the certainty that God has appointed something to happen through us. We don't have to expedite it nor do we have to make a prophecy be fulfilled.

CHAPTER FIVE

BECOMING HIS HANDS EXTENDED TO HEAL

FOR I KNOW THAT THIS WILL TURN OUT FOR MY DELIVERANCE THROUGH YOUR PRAYER AND THE SUPPLY OF THE SPIRIT OF JESUS CHRIST. (PHILIPPIANS 1:19)

Being the "middle man" of hope

When He had come down from the mountain, great multitudes followed Him. And behold, a leper came and worshiped Him, saying, "Lord, if You are willing, You can make me clean."

Then Jesus put out His hand and touched him, saying, "I am willing; be cleansed." Immediately his leprosy was cleansed.

And Jesus said to him, "See that you tell no one; but go your way, show yourself to the priest, and offer the gift that Moses commanded, as a testimony to them."

Now when Jesus had entered Capernaum, a centurion came to Him, pleading with Him, saying, "Lord, my servant is lying at home paralyzed, dreadfully tormented."

And Jesus said to him, "I will come and heal him."

The centurion answered and said, "Lord, I am not worthy that You should come under my roof. But only speak a word, and my servant will be healed. For I also am a man under authority, having soldiers under me. And I say to this one, 'Go,' and he goes; and to another, 'Come,' and he comes; and to my servant, 'Do this,' and he does it."

When Jesus heard it, He marveled, and said to those who followed, "Assuredly, I say to you, I have not found such great faith, not even in Israel! And I say to you that many will come from east and west, and sit down with Abraham, Isaac, and Jacob in the Kingdom of heaven. But the sons of the kingdom will be cast out into outer darkness. There will be weeping and gnashing of teeth." Then Jesus said to the centurion, "Go your way; and as you have believed, so let it be done for you." And his servant was healed at that same hour.

Now when Jesus had come into Peter's house, He saw his wife's mother lying sick with a fever. So, He touched her hand, and the fever left her. And she arose and served them. (Matthew 8:1-15)

As we read through Matthew 8, we learn the healing ministry of Jesus Christ is a fulfillment of prophesy. As we can recall, Isaiah 53:4 promised that He Himself would take our infirmities and bear our sicknesses. The focal point of this study isn't only the fact that Jesus heals, but that He wants to use us as the agency through which His healing power flows. When Jesus heals, what we do with that healing is just as important to the Lord as when we've received it. God isn't going to randomly heal people who use their life for self-destruction or for ruining other people's lives. We can't live any old way and think that God has to pick up the pieces after we've made a wreck of our bodies. Yet, even then, our loving Father intervenes. When we come to Jesus He works deliverance; often bringing a new hope and new lease on life. But what we do with our life after being healed is also very important.

- **Healed and serving** – In Matthew 8:14-15, we read that Peter's mother-in-law was sick with a fever. It took but a touch from Jesus to make her well; then she arose and saw to the needs of all those present. Her healing was a springboard to serving others.

- **When Jesus touches us** – When Jesus touches us and we're healed, we can believe He has the ability to touch other difficulties in our lives, too. We become people who understand and who receive the dimensions of His power.

There are two important principles involved here:

- When the Lord touches one particular area of our life, we mustn't limit His reach. He can touch other areas of difficulty, as well.

- We can be the "middle man," the significant person who makes a difference whether or not the healing flow comes to someone. Our example is the centurion in Matthew 8.

The word of faith

Matthew 8:3-13 is often used to teach one of the great power principles of the Bible. That principle is called "the word of faith." It's knowing that what God says is true. It rules and overrules any circumstance where we abide in that faith. Circumstances don't matter; it's in the Spirit of the love of God and the compassion of Christ that ministers those things. This principle is still in effect, even when the word of faith that we confess doesn't seem to work out the way we wanted. This isn't because God backed down on His word, but because we didn't properly understand how to apply the key to the circumstance.

The centurion and his servant

We learn in Matthew 8:13, that the servant was healed the same hour that Jesus said to the Centurion, "Go your way and as you have believed, so let it be done for you." We find nothing in the text that says the servant did anything before his healing happened. There's one significant point, though. The Centurion mentioned that this servant was faithful in doing all he was told to do (Matthew 8:9); his faithfulness touched his master's heart. The wholeness which came to the servant was actually the glorious product of what someone else did. A powerful display of God's grace and healing came because the centurion was willing to be an instrument of intervention and because of his faith in God.

God is willing

It is God's will to deliver. His will is to fill. His will is to save and to heal. Jesus said, "I will come and heal him." (Matthew 8:7) Here again is the divine affirmation that God was ready to heal. Jesus is the image of the Father's will in everything He did in ministry. The fullness of the Father is manifest in Him. Jesus always responds to the call for help and brings healing. Anything short of this has to do with our incapacity to receive all that God has to give. Sometimes healing is immediate, and in other instances it takes time, but that doesn't mean it won't happen. Our responsibility is to be open to it.

Rejecting tradition

Jesus marveled at the centurion's faith when he said, "Only speak a word and my servant will be healed." (Matthew 8:8) This Roman soldier recognized Jesus functioned in unlimited authority. Nothing, therefore, was outside the arena of possibility. Two things are notable in this story: his rejection of social tradition, and his recognition of Jesus' power. A Roman didn't go to a Jew for any reason, because Jews were subjugated by Romans. On the other hand, Jews didn't have anything to do with Romans, either. Both the centurion and Jesus rejected the norm for a healing breakthrough.

Becoming instruments of God

When we recognize Jesus had the situation within His domain of operation, we can become instruments which release the power of God. We must understand that Jesus can and will work healing in people. Jesus searches for an agent or middleman who can receive something for someone else. It takes more than just people who know how to speak the word of faith, though. There's a compassion, which moves us into action. In this case, the master broke social tradition and sought help because his servant was "dreadfully tormented."

Social traditions are not where it's at

The centurion came to Jesus, violating all that he was taught. There needs to be a certain breaking with tradition in every one of us. We need to be willing to upset our own ideology, then open up to a flow of compassion. By believing that the word of Jesus Christ is powerful in any situation, we become agents of that flow to people. We must believe that His ministry is divine in nature and beyond the ordinary.

Divine healing

The power of the Lord Jesus Christ can heal the sick and afflicted when we believe in prayer. It's not just a matter of human effort, formulas, sloganeering, or incantations spoken in repetition until finally we believe. We're talking about the promises of God where those things are entrusted to the church to live, experience and minister. Divine healing is a matter of people being healed and made well by the power of Jesus Christ according to God's word ministered in His love.

Are you willing?

Until the church of Jesus Christ learns how to be the agency by which the Lord works, there'll be a lot of sickness prevailing in this world. The paralytic in Luke 5:16-20 was carried to Jesus by his friends. We can find paralytics in so many parts of life – those whose lives are falling apart because they're physically, emotionally, or sociologically crippled. Sickness can't survive when people decide to break with tradition, reject social convention and let compassion fill their hearts. When we come to the Savior to receive from Him that one who is of a distance and believe Him for the flow of life in that person, we will be His agents and instruments of healing.

Sometimes people think they don't want to bother Jesus for His provisions. There are others who don't move into action because they just don't want to bother doing it, or aren't even bothered by it. When you're willing to be bothered or inconvenienced, that is called "ministry." You will move into the liberty of seeing the power of God pass from you to someone else. There's healing in the Name and touch of Jesus, but we must be the ones who touch others, allowing His love to flow through us. For the love of God to flow, it flows on the basis of people who believe that the word of Jesus Christ is all powerful, and believe the will of God is to minister wholeness and are available to whatever inconvenience is involved on their part. We're to be willing to see the truth in being a channel of the healing life of Jesus.

One particular man of God was on his knees, desperately beseeching God about a particular situation saying, "Work by Your power! Lord, work and move by Your power!" Time and again, he presented this before the Lord. Then suddenly the still, small voice of the Holy Spirit interrupted him with these words, "Son, I work by my love." When we let God break in to do what He wants, putting our own thoughts aside about how He should or will do it, He does it! You see, people aren't healed by mechanically spouting scriptures, people are healed by people who minister the Word in love."

Get to know God's heart for the hurting

At evening, when the sun had set, they brought to Him all who were sick and those who were demon-possessed. And the whole city was gathered together at the door. Then He healed many who were sick with various diseases, and cast out many demons; and HE did not allow the demons to speak, because they knew Him.
(Mark 1:32-34)

Mark's Gospel characterizes Jesus Christ as "God's Servant," which is the most likely reason that Mark did not include the genealogy of Jesus. Mark's writing is rife with details on the setting, the activities that Jesus conducted and the response from those to whom he ministered. The text indicates the people came to Jesus after the end of the Sabbath, when there were no restrictions on travel and activity. Jesus ministered to the whole city at night; healing the sick and casting out demons (while forbidding them to speak). This recounting of Jesus, working at night to meet the needs of a whole city, clearly depicts him as God's Servant Who came to reflect the Father's heart for those who are hurting.

Most everyone in our world today is hurting to one degree or another, having to face things that are painful. There was an old song from the early 1970's, *Alone Again*, that, forty-five years later, people in a rather broad demographic still remember and relate. A line in the song states, "It seems to me that there are more hearts broken in the world than can be mended, what shall we do...." It is a fact that so many people really do hurt.

Jesus spoke and commanded the unclean

spirit to be quiet and come out of the man. Parapsychologists today indicate there is something we can't define that influences people toward aberrant behavior. Some speculate that this "something we can't define" is a personification of evil that drives people into alcohol and drug abuse, anger, hatred and lust that splinter homes and other relationships. We cannot biomedically solve all the emotional and mental problems represented in our population. These are unclean spirits, the dirt of hell being shoveled on us. Jesus Christ is the One Who can cast out spirits and silence their influence on our lives. He is God's Servant, and only begotten Son who came to earth to reflect God's heart for those who are hurting. He does heal because He alone has overcome the evil one through the finished work of the Cross.

Christ brings purpose into our lives

When Jesus started to call His disciples, they were men who had jobs, but no purpose. He called them into the Heavenly Father's purpose with His invitation of, "Follow Me!" Jesus can bring meaning to our jobs, bringing those jobs into the Father's purpose through personal revelation.

Jesus' power delivers us from the influence of unclean spirits

We are in the last days, and demonic influence is rampant internationally, nationally and in our communities. No matter what name is given to the upswing of evil, it cannot be tamed by analysis. It can only be tamed by the power of the living God. We were created to know the function of God's holy purpose. Thoughts that are out of control and contrary to the ways of God—thoughts one wishes they could alter—can only be broken through the power of God. It is Jesus Who can break the darkness.

Jesus comes to us as healer

Upon leaving the synagogue on the Sabbath, Jesus went to the house of Simon and Andrew, where Simon's mother-in-law was sick with a fever. They told Jesus about her, and he took her hand and helped her up. The fever left and she began to prepare food for them. Jesus comes to us as healer; whatever the physical situation, he heals the heart of the hurting.

Jesus touches the untouchable

The last story in the first chapter of Mark is the man with leprosy who came to Jesus. He begged Him, saying "If you are willing, you can make me clean." Lepers were the incurable of that time, similar to HIV/AIDS patients today. Lepers were castaways—it was illegal to touch a leper for the perceived protection of the population. Jesus' response to this leper's request for healing was to say, "I will." This healing event is for us—it is God's will for us to be healed.

Jesus is a reality answer

The touching of the leper is the evidence of his will to touch you and me. Jesus' response to the leper, a societal untouchable, was "I will," meaning, I will lift you up, touch you, heal you and give you purpose. Jesus is the One Who can cast out spirits and silence their influence on our lives. He is God's Servant. He came to earth to reflect God's heart for those who are hurting and he does heal because he has overcome the evil one. The touching of the leper is the evidence of His will to touch you and me."

Touched by the finger of God

For God has not given us a spirit of fear, but of power and of love and of a sound mind.
(2 Timothy 1:7)

And He was casting out a demon, and it was mute. So, it was, when the demon had gone out, that the mute spoke; and the multitudes marveled. But some of them said, "He casts out demons by Beelzebub, the ruler of the demons."

Others, testing Him, sought from Him a sign from heaven. But He, knowing their thoughts, said to them: "Every kingdom divided against itself is brought to desolation, and a house divided against itself falls. If Satan also is divided against himself, how will his kingdom stand? Because you say I cast out demons by Beelzebub. And if I cast out demons by Beelzebub, by whom do your sons cast them out? Therefore, they will be your judges. But if I cast out demons with the finger of God, surely the kingdom of God has come upon you. When a strong man, fully armed, guards his own palace, his goods are in peace. But when a stronger than he comes upon him and overcomes him, he takes from him all his armor in which he is trusted, and divides his spoils. He who is not with Me is against Me, and he who does not gather with me scatters.

"When an unclean spirit goes out of a man, he goes through dry places, seeking rest; and finding none, he says, 'I will return to my house from which I came.' And when he comes, he finds it swept and put in order. Then he goes and takes with him seven other spirits more wicked than himself, and they enter and dwell there; and the last state of that man is worse than the first."
(Luke 11:14-26)

It was normal for Jesus to directly confront the powers of hell head-on and to cast out demons (verse 14). Response to that was not only amazement (verse 14), but also criticism (verse 15) and challenge (verse 16). Although Jesus conveyed to the church the ministry of deliverance, there's always been something in the religious mindset of "churchianity" that would rather theorize, intellectualize, and memorize the Scripture than see it actualized. We are dealing with more than the intellectual idea that Jesus is greater than the powers of darkness. Salvation is not what is at issue here, but possessing our inheritance of full victory at every part of our being in Christ. This is a growing and maturing experience which takes time and patience. As with Israel, who was given the whole territory but possessed it a piece at a time, so it is with believers and the unfolding dimensions of realizing God's kingdom in us.

They sought a sign

There are always people who don't reject what you're doing, but want to see you do it again – on somebody else. It is a fundamental, intellectual acknowledgement that a ministry exists, but a refusal to submit yourself to it. That's true of many believers who don't want to come to terms with the possibility that Jesus wants to deal with them more thoroughly.

The King and the Kingdom had come

Jesus was not explaining the obvious that if an army has traitors, it can't win the war (verse 17). He was answering a society who had never before experienced the entry of the power of the Kingdom of God confronting the kingdom of darkness. Wherever the King comes to move in human experience, then the kingdom intrudes itself to fill all the available territory surrendered unto that kingdom rule.

Jesus explains a new authority was now here in the human arena, not one that bargains with evil in an attempt at a truce (that's characteristic of humanity), acknowledging an invisible realm of satanic power that opposes man, then trying to appease the demons with ritual.

Jesus was also pointing out that His kingdom wasn't merely pacifying people with the best that human reason (psychology) or medicine could provide. Mere man does work sincerely at deliverance programs such as counseling and medical treatment, but a "measure of success" is the best those programs can ever do.

Jesus says you no longer have to (a) Bargain with the realm of darkness to try to arrive at a truce; or (b) Buy the "measure of release" man can provide because genuine liberation comes freely by the power of the living God.

God only needs to use His finger against a flea like Satan

The Holy Spirit is cast into the likeness of God's finger doing two things:

- Coming to point out in our lives any place where the Lord can make us free; and

- Casting out the controlling powers of hell. It's as though Jesus is saying when God comes to deal with the liberation process in our lives (confronting the hellish works of darkness) He doesn't need His whole arm; He doesn't even need His whole hand—by His finger He flicks out the powers of hell.

Will you let the Lord point His finger in your Life? The finger of God casts out that which has enthroned itself in your life. Is there any place in your life where there is another power than the rule of the Lord that sits in control? The casting out is not from one's body or mind; it is a casting of that other power out of a place of control in our lives.

Jesus speaks of Himself as the "stronger"

(verse 22) and Satan as the one who "scatters" (verse 23) who does anything he can to dissipate, confuse and destroy life. When the kingdom comes, the finger of God points out those things we must deal with in our lives. We must:

- Be convinced we're dealing with reality, not a superstition.
- Invite His rule and authority without fear.
- Allow Him to "finger" the issues—point them out.

After any work of hell is removed, there needs to be a fullness of the Spirit of God (verses 24-26) in its place. Sadly, some believers will tolerate areas of bondage in their lives because they can't imagine themselves any other way. But Jesus can. Jesus can! These people identify with their bondage rather than in the potential of liberty Christ has for them.

So, if you get free, your only living option is to let Jesus fill that part of your life. There are believers in Christ who would rather tolerate a place of bondage in their life than surrender to the full flow of the Holy Spirit in that area. A dear woman whom I pastored some years ago did exactly what I am now writing about in this book.

She was set free by the finger of God, and my dear friend, He can do the same for you. Here is her testimony:

There was something wrong. Very wrong. I was twenty-nine years old and I should have felt happy. I had been happily married for seven years, had three adorable children and had been living in the dream home I had designed for several months, but I felt nothing. I didn't feel happy and I didn't feel sad, I didn't feel anything at all. I did not know why, but something deep inside told me something was horribly wrong, and I was right.

A few months later, I had my first flashback. I had no idea I had been sexually abused as a child, but that is what I experienced in the memory. There was not a face; only body parts. My husband held me as I sobbed. After I calmed down, information came to me. "I would never accuse anyone of something like this without seeing who is was, but everything inside says that it is my dad and my mom knows."

I did not understand at the time that the information was coming from clarity deep inside, and that God would reveal my abuse to me in layers that I could grasp, one at a time. It would be a pace that God could heal me and the only way I would not be destroyed in the process. That is just the way God works. Unfortunately, it took a long time for me to stop fighting the pace and process and begin to just listen.

My husband and I began a journey that day that would last for the next twenty years. For a long nine months, I fought the flashbacks of abuse. It was not long before my dad's face did indeed show up in the memories. One memory even included my mom entering the room as my dad was on top of me. He growled at her to get out. She clenched her fists, turned and left. The information was correct: it was my dad, and my mom knew. Now I had some credibility with myself that the information coming to me from somewhere inside should be trusted.

It would be assumed that having the flashbacks and legitimizing them would give me some emotional release, but I was inexplicably getting worse. We gave up, and off I went to an outpatient Christian clinic for some help. The sweet psychiatrist became my champion and gave me the strength to keep going and not give up. I went back to my family and hoped things were about to get better. They quickly got worse.

Terrifying fear gripped me. I could not

function. I was crying day and night, barely able to care for my young and confused children. My husband was flummoxed and we did not know what to do. We kept crying out to God to help us, to explain what was going on.

Finally, I started getting sounds of chanting. I saw candles and smelled smoke. I saw people with black grim reaper like robes with the hoods covering their faces in shadows. I was young and I was in pain.

I had no reference for this. I never liked the horror movies or anything with witchcraft in it. I had been a Christian my entire life. Saved at seven and filled with the Holy Spirit at twelve, I knew to stay away from the demonic. I wanted nothing to do with it.

My husband thought the flashbacks had to do with something called ritual abuse. We really did not know much about it and we looked at the books about it at the library, but they looked too scary to even read. We decided to just wait to see what would transpire.

The memories came for the next fifteen years. At first, they were in rapid succession. I was very young, and I was the focus of sexual torture mixed with Christianity and the occult. I would be in the center of a circle of the robed adults and that meant that I was going to be in agonizing pain. The pain would always come first in a flashback. For several days I would be in pain wondering how in the world it could hurt where it was and what could cause that pain. A few days later, the rest of the memory would come, seeing it through my eyes. The scenario would fit the pain exactly.

I did not want to believe that I was a survivor of what I would later find out was called "Satanic Ritual Abuse" or SRA. Back to the outpatient clinic we went. The kind psychiatrist listened carefully as I explained what was going on. He shocked me be telling him that he had already known that I was an SRA survivor. He said that the level of torture my dad had exerted on me in the home sexual abuse was in the top ninetieth percentile of severity. It took a long time for me to take that in. I was on this journey and there was no getting out of it. I was an SRA survivor.

God kept me on the path I daily fought because He knew that it was the path of healing. Eventually he put me in contact with other survivors and I found out that what happened to me was exactly like what happened to them, and there were survivors world-wide.

The tricky part of my recovery was spiritual healing. I found a Christian counselor who had Theophostic therapy where we would travel back to each memory and put God in the center of it. We would look for what He would say about it.

I realized with amazement that God was there during my abuse. Right in the middle of where the devil had more control than anywhere in society, where people were trying to please him and do what he wanted them to do, God was there! They were making a mockery out of everything to do with Jesus and God was right there making a way for me to get through it. Night after night, year after year, He was there. He watched what they did. He got me through to the next morning and then was with me as I got out of bed and faced another day. He gave me one day after another until he could get me away to college and finally into the arms of a godly husband. He saw ahead to a life outside of abuse and a life spent with knowing God and loving Him. When I wanted to die and not be abused anymore, He kept me going because He saw my future.

I can say with absolute certainly that only God could save me, deliver me, heal me and use me. There was nothing of me that earned it. It

was freely given, and it is much appreciated. I could not be here today without the goodness of God in the land of the living. What the devil meant for my total destruction, God turned into a miracle. God is truly greater than anything that was thrown against me. God is good!
    -L.M.

As we close this little book on deliverance, my prayer is that it has been most helpful and a blessing to you. I have endeavored to create a relatively short, concise, and easy-to-read guide on this very important subject. I would like to now lead you in a prayer of deliverance. Pray it aloud and with all your heart. Believe, speak, receive and stand upon it in Jesus' Name and continue to do so through your peaks and valleys. Victory is within your reach, loved one. By faith, take hold of it now!

You pray:

Abba Father, I ask You to forgive me for all of my sin. I ask You to release me from every bondage, in Jesus' Name. Amen.

    Now I pray for the precious person reading this book. Lord, by the authority You've given me,

I take authority over Satan. I address every demonic spirit that's held my brothers and sisters bound, and I command you to go, in Jesus' Name. It is not my authority, but it is the authority of the Lord Jesus Christ. My brothers and sisters are covered by the blood of the Lamb; they overcome by the word of their testimony. They are born again; not of corruptible seed but incorruptible, which lives and abides forever. The angels which are mighty in strength watch over Your Word to perform it. The Word of God is living and active. It is sharper than any two-edged sword. It's sweeter than honey and purer than gold, and His Name is "The Word of God" and by the Word and the blood of the Lamb we are set free today.

We take authority over every spirit of bitterness, unforgiveness, resentment, hate, malice, envy or jealousy and command you to go now, in the Name of Jesus. I rebuke every spirit of insecurity or inferiority, fear, rejection, self-hate, self-pity, self-destruction, in Jesus' Name. Suicide, we command you to go now in Jesus' Name.

Every spirit of anger, rage, murder, or violence, or lawlessness, we command you to go in Jesus' Name.

Every spirit of sexual immorality, impurity, adultery, fornication, lust, pornography, and all forms of sexual impurity, I command you to go in Jesus' Name.

Every spirit of pride, or lying, every Jezebel spirit, rebellion, deception, manipulation, control, I command you to go in the Name of Jesus. Every spirit of criticism, judgmentalism, arrogance, prejudice, or racism, I command you to go in Jesus' Name.

Every spirit of greed, materialism, selfishness, covetousness, selfish ambition, I command you to go in Jesus' Name.

Depression, anxiety, worry, suicide, you must go in Jesus' Name.

Addiction, alcoholism, drunkenness, drugs, gluttony, you must flee in Jesus' Name.

Every spirit of legalism, or religious pride, or heresy, false doctrine, we command you to go in the Name of Jesus.

Every spirit of stealing, laziness, slothfulness, unbelief, rebellion against authority, go in Jesus' Name.

Every spirit of guilt, shame, embarrassment, humiliation, you get out in Jesus' Name.

Every spirit of sickness, disease, infirmity,

chronic health issues, you must go in Jesus' Name.

Every spirit of witchcraft, the occult, blasphemy, we command you to go in Jesus' Name. We break every word curse and spell spoken against us in Jesus' Name. Every generational curse, I command you to flee in the Name of Jesus. Every demonic spirit that has held by brothers and sisters in bondage, I command you to go right now in Jesus' Name. Amen!

Now say after me: Lord, I receive the Holy Spirit, and will You fill me with the Holy Spirit every place where evil spirits have left? Will You fill me with Your Spirit now? I receive You now, and my freedom, in Jesus' Name I pray. Amen!

Reference

Prayer inspired by contents of the book, *Truly Free: Breaking the Snares that so Easily Entangle* by Robert Morris, published by Thomas Nelson, 2015.

ABOUT THE AUTHOR

Rev. Anthony Sluzas is a traveling evangelist
and revivalist. He is the
founder of Your Place Of
Grace Ministries. His
testimony is one of
deliverance from emotional
and physical abuse which he
experienced as a child in
parochial school, and
substance abuse as a young aspiring
actor/musician in Hollywood. While there,
Anthony played several tiny bits on the sitcoms,
Three's Company, The Two of Us, and appeared
in numerous live theatrical productions.

He crashed and burned emotionally and
spiritually in 1987, but the following year
experienced a radical transformation in his
heart and life when he accepted Jesus as his
Lord and Savior while listening to E.V. Hill on
TBN. God has worked miracles in Anthony's life
and He can do the same for anyone and everyone
through Jesus Christ.

Anthony served as lead Pastor in several
Assemblies of God churches from 1994-2010.
Since 2010, Anthony has ministered from

America's east coast to west coast and points in between. Anthony preaches and teaches the Message of Grace and Faith through the Cross of Christ. He is called to win souls for Christ, and he focuses on God's Word in the areas of forgiveness, healing and deliverance. Anthony loves to serve pastors, no matter the denomination, through prayer and a hand of friendship because he too was a pastor for years. Now, for the past decade years, Anthony Sluzas has worked as a traveling evangelist and revivalist. His heart's desire is to minister to and point the way for those whom the world considers "lost causes" just like he was, to the Lord Jesus Christ.

For more information about Your Place of Grace Ministries, visit Anthony Sluzas' website at YOURPLACEOFGRACE.COM. Also, be sure to download the "Your Place of Grace" app, available in both the apple and Google play stores online.

personal values

personal

values

God's Game Plan
for Life

Kurt Senske

Augsburg Books
MINNEAPOLIS

For Laurie and Sydney

contents

acknowledgments

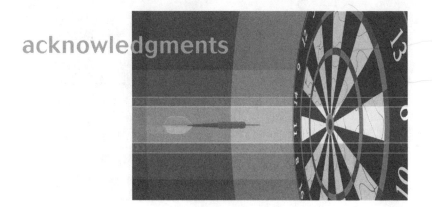

My education in leading a life of personal values fortunately began at home. My sister, Susan, and I are forever indebted to our parents, Al and Ruth Senske, who were and continue to be role models, teachers, mentors, and friends. Their love, patience, and instruction is reflected throughout this book.

My wife, Laurie, and daughter, Sydney, keep me focused on what is truly important. Laurie's strong faith and unwavering support has added health to my physical, mental, and spiritual life. Sydney's sense of humor, unquestioning faith, and constant quest for adventure open my eyes and heart to new possibilities. Together we strive to use our partnership and family life as a vehicle to share our many blessings with others.

I am also blessed to be centered in a caring extended family. Bill and Barbara Lawler go beyond the call of duty in caring for their grateful son-in-law. I also deeply appreciate the love and support of Susan, John, Lisa, D.J., Krista, Paul, Mark, Kenny, Katy, Kirby, and Annie. They are effective witnesses through their faith and daily living.

Rev. Stephen Wenk provided both theological clarity and countless useful suggestions while critiquing an early draft of this manuscript. Stephen's passion for caring for others is evident through his servant-leader persona. He is both a role model and a friend. I also owe a debt of gratitude to Rich Bimler, Rick Herman, Doug Anderson, Jack Fortin, and a host of others who took time to explore with me the topic of this book. My trusted and loyal assistant, Karen Ashorn, went beyond the call of duty in proofreading the manuscript and correcting my footnotes. This book would remain unfinished if not for her assistance. Finally, I am grateful for a sabbatical that the Board of Directors of Lutheran Social Services provided that allowed me to finish this book. Their values-based approach to governance has added lasting value to our organization.

And last, but not least, I thank you for trusting me enough to take seriously my Christ-based framework for living. My hope and prayer is that together we can continue to make a difference in the lives of others through our personal and professional callings. I look forward to continuing this journey with you today and, God willing, for years to come.

Kurt Senske
Austin, Texas
Summer 2004

introduction

If a man cannot be a Christian where he is, he cannot be a Christian anywhere.

—Henry Ward Beecher

Being a Christian is difficult: it requires obedience without full understanding and faith without full knowledge; one foot in the temporal world with the other dangling in eternity; self-sacrifice for the greater good; standing tall to the temptations of the world; humbleness in the midst of success; quiet strength in the face of ridicule; and the search for justice in an unjust world.

Living in the twenty-first century is also difficult. Paradoxically, we live in a time of abundance, but never feel we have enough. We enjoy all the modern necessities of life but die far too young of such stress-related diseases as heart attacks, strokes, and cancer. We have virtually all of the world's information at our fingertips, but don't know how to apply these megabytes of data to enhance our personal lives. We desire close familial relationships but have a hard time tolerating those we say we love. We want to serve others but cannot get beyond our sinful self-centeredness. We feel an unfulfilled, intense spiritual hunger but treat our involvement in the church as just another civic affiliation, social gathering, or family tradition. We long to live a life of significance but choose monetary rewards over purposeful callings. We say we want to follow in Jesus's path, but our actions don't always match our intentions.

Living a twenty-first century Christian life is difficult. During the past decade, economic circumstances have shaken our collective faith in humanity and its capacity to act with integrity to its core. On a corporate level we have seen that organizations like Enron, WorldCom, the Roman Catholic Church, Arthur Andersen, and Tyco have failed to provide moral leadership and have caused untold suffering to millions. On a political level we witness a president lie about his affair with a young intern, and countless politicians sell out the public for personal gain. Both within and beyond our borders we witness horrific acts of brutality through suicide bombings, weapons of mass destruction, and the inevitable tit-for-tat retaliation. Closer to home, we see broken families, drug and alcohol abuse, and children who seem distant. At work, we watch others get ahead by acting unethically; at times we even cut corners ourselves, justifying our actions by telling ourselves, "Everyone else is doing it, why shouldn't I?" Personally, we watch with dismay as our children fail to adopt the values we tell them are important, but fail to demonstrate ourselves.

Sadly, many self-professed Christians don't act like Christians. This has far-reaching tragic societal and personal consequences. Although we cannot judge the souls of others, Rev. Billy Graham states that, "[M]illions of professing Christians are only 'professing.' They do not enjoy a genuine relationship with Christ. They live lives characterized by the flesh, and will go into eternity thinking they are saved by virtue of their membership in a congregation."[1] Strong words for each of us to wrestle with.

Our stress-filled, frantic pace has overtaken our brief search for understanding. Being a Christian then becomes one of many items we cross off our "to do" list; we quickly forget about it on Monday as we move on to the next task. Our churches often promote this compartmentalization when they make it easy for us to fulfill our "duty" without being horribly inconvenienced. Taken to the extreme, some even offer streaming-video services so we can watch our pastor "live" from our bed on Sunday morning. What results is a lifestyle that allows us to fulfill our Christian obligation without realizing that it is our faith that provides us with a key to unlocking a life of meaning. What results are individuals such as Erin Polzin, a twenty-year-old college student who listens to worship on the radio, confesses online, and tithes via PayPal, an online payment service. Her comments may well reflect the sentiments of many: "I don't like getting up early on Sundays. This is like going to church without really having to."[2]

Being a Christian is difficult, and I am not immune. I was once a player in this crowd—a fairly regular attendee of church on Sunday, but with little else to show the other six days of the week. Oh, I could fake it well when it was in my interest to do so, but it wasn't genuine. I never found playing this role particularly fulfilling. It was little more than an insurance policy in case heaven did, in fact, exist; it was nice to have in my back pocket on the day of my death, but didn't play the leading role in my life. That spot was reserved for my other roles: attorney, athlete, party-goer, political animal, administrator, writer, and overachiever. Although I did obtain earthly success, deep down I knew something was missing. I knew that in order to be truly happy, I had to change my game plan. I still play most of those other roles, but the new and only leading role in my earthly production is that of being a Christian—one who lives through and for God.

Having been trained as an attorney and as a social scientist, I have a brain wired to assess life analytically and empirically. At times, this has hindered my relationship with God. I have difficulty measuring my faith. I cannot touch or see it. Although I sometimes can "feel" it, I wonder if my mind is playing a trick on my emotions. I cannot point to a specific date when I was "born again." In my faith tradition, that happened at my baptism. Since then, my growth in faith has been a gradual process. Over the past forty-four years the Holy Spirit has used literally hundreds of people from all walks of life to bring me to where I am today—at peace with God and myself, and leading a life of significance, health, and balance.

Looking back, I realize how the Holy Spirit has worked through my own efforts to incorporate my faith into all aspects of my life, bringing both intended and unintended consequences. Following what I call God's Game Plan for Life has brought me closer to God, strengthened my family relationships, and, in a small way, added value to my community, my nation, and the world in which I live. I have also become healthier—physically, mentally, and spiritually. It has allowed me to separate the important from the trivial, which has added balance and significance to my life.

I am a man of God. I am also still hard-wired as an attorney and social scientist, akin to *Dragnet's* Sergeant Friday who said, "Just the facts, Ma'am." In order to satisfy my need for the facts, I began searching for causal relationships and data that would provide evidence of the connection between incorporating my faith into all aspects of my life and feeling more significant and happier. What has resulted from this journey is *Personal Values: God's Game Plan for Life.* It is my prayer that what has worked in my life—and in the lives of countless others—will also be a resource in creating your own personal Game Plan for Life.

The idea of putting my findings in writing first came to me after I had written *Executive Values: A Christian Approach to Organizational Leadership.*[3] In *Executive Values* I demonstrate empirically a cause-and-effect relationship between adhering to one's values and organizational success; how, by following the golden rule of leadership, one can do *well* by doing *good*; and that biblically based values enable us to succeed.

As I traveled throughout the country talking about *Executive Values,* I had an opportunity to listen to the personal stories of many whom I met along the way. These stories can be broadly divided into two common themes. The first involved people who were utterly discouraged and were losing faith in what it meant to live out their Christian principles in a post-modern world. Time after time they observed self-professed "Christians" acting unethically when they were "away from church." Christian Harrison spent twenty-two years of his professional life as an attorney—most of that time as a state and federal prosecutor. As a U.S. attorney, he prosecuted some 150 public officials in East Texas, including judges, sheriffs, county commissioners, and other law enforcement officials. Their crimes included racketeering, arson, and murder. They enriched themselves by taking kickbacks and running protective monopolies for drug and liquor rings, gambling establishments, and houses of prostitution. As a prosecutor, Harrison wasn't surprised that people gave in to the temptations of greed and selfish pride. What shook his faith was a discovery that he made in reviewing the pre-sentencing reports prepared by the Federal Probation Office. The reports revealed that, almost to a person, the defendants were elders and deacons in their churches. They showed up in church every Sunday, but the rest of the week lived in a way that had no connection to the values they were taught there.[4]

Another group of conversations revolved around whether or not the framework laid out in *Executive Values* could be incorporated into our daily living. Those with whom I spoke were Christians who, like myself, struggled over how to live out their faith 24 hours a day, 365 days a year. What I found fascinating were the three common threads that emerged: how to navigate today's ethical minefields and incorporate our faith into our daily life in order to live a God-pleasing life of significance; how to maintain our health in order to lead a long, vigorous, and enjoyable life; and how to balance our life in order to serve properly our family, church, community, and work.

These conversations were with people of all walks of life and ages—business executives, high school and college students, professionals, homemakers, hourly employees, and retirees. They were rich and poor, old and young, male and female. All desired to live a God-pleasing life of significance, health, and balance, but had a gnawing feeling that they weren't quite getting it right. They were attempting to strengthen their faith, but struggled over how life in the twenty-first century fit into their admittedly weak relationship with God. Many (including myself, at times) were frenzied, stressed, and barely in control.

I began this journey some twenty years ago to seek answers about the meaning of life. I was living in Paris at the time—a place conducive to reading important books and thinking great thoughts at street-side cafes. On my mind were such questions as: What is my role here on earth? What does God want me to do with my life? How do I incorporate five-thousand-year-old biblical principles into postmodern life? Why, despite my best intentions, do I keep screwing up? Why is it so hard not to be self-centered? How can I lead a life of significance, health, and balance? Is there, in fact, a God and a Savior who died for my sins?

It would be a mistake to think that I am an expert on personal values. (Although, if it is true that you learn from your mistakes, then indeed maybe I am.) I am all too well aware that I am no better—and probably not even as good—a person as you. I am not a theologian. I am merely a humble, broken Christian trying faithfully to serve God in a sinful world.

Having now made full, although vague, disclosure, I am convinced that this book can be of great benefit to you, because I possess firsthand knowledge of how implementing God's Game Plan for Life has had on my life, as well as on the lives of others who adhere to it.

Personal Values doesn't attempt to tell you what specific decisions you must make in order to lead a God-pleasing life. You must make those decisions for yourself. I cannot tell you whether or not it is ethical to drive an SUV, if you should tithe, that you must be a Republican or Democrat, if it's okay to own a second home at the beach, whether you should take a more prestigious job that will mean more time away from your family, whether you should agree to serve on yet another church committee, whether it is ethical to hunt animals for sport, if it's okay to invest in tobacco stocks or gamble at casinos, whether to leave an abusive spouse, or whether it's okay to go eight miles above the speed limit. Rather, *Personal Values* provides a biblically based, empirically proven framework that will help you find significance in your daily work, balance in your family life, and improved physical, mental, and spiritual health. This book will also provide you with a framework to better serve your family, neighbors, coworkers, congregation, community, nation, and world. *Personal Values* is unique in that it incorporates these findings into the larger story of who we are and why we are placed on this earth at this particular time. It provides the context and reason for living.

Personal Values is different from many self-help books in that it underscores the relationship between one's ethical behavior and one's health. Martin Luther addressed this relationship:

> The Christian should be guided by this one thing alone that he may serve and benefit others in all that he does, considering nothing except the need and the advantage of his neighbor. . . . This is what makes caring for the body a Christian work, that through its health and comfort we may be able to work, to acquire and lay by funds with which to aid those who are in need, that in this way the stronger member may serve the weaker. . . . This is a truly Christian life. Here faith is active in love.[5]

What the Bible tells us, and what research demonstrates, is that by serving others, *we* become healthier. The more we care for others, the more we take care of ourselves.

Personal Values is written from a Christian perspective because that is who I am. You do not, however, have to be a Christian to benefit from this framework. The connection articulated here applies equally to believers and nonbelievers. It is my belief, however, that our faith enables us to take this Game Plan for Life to an even higher plane. On this plane where we enjoy a relationship with God that—despite our frailties and failures—assures us that we live in grace now and into eternity. This assurance is what gives inner peace.

I began this introspective journey by devouring the wide array of religious and secular self-help literature currently on the market. I was dizzied by the titles promising you can lose weight, look good, live forever, dress for success, find your dream job, locate your inner being and spiritual side, simplify your life, and meditate your way to peace. Along the way, I also met some new literary friends and personal heroes. Dietrich Bonhoeffer, Francis of Assisi, Derrick Bell, Rick Warren, J. Heinrich Arnold, Henri Nouwen, C. S. Lewis, and Parker Palmer come to mind. Most importantly, I went back to the original source, the Bible, to refresh my memory of what God has to say about living out our earthly lives. I also examined the scientific research to find out what the medical community had to say about the correlation between adhering to one's values and leading a life of significance, health, and balance.

To my surprise, I found a wealth of empirical data that substantiates the biblical instructions of how to live a life of significance. Just as the empirical data provided in *Executive Values* demonstrates that our biblically based values allow us to do well organizationally, *Personal Values* describes how such data confirms my belief that adhering to our personal values will lead us to a life of significance. In addition to sharing my story, I share the stories of others—many of whom have implemented the Game Plan for Life far better than I. These are, in most cases, simple, ordinary people like you and me. They all make mistakes, some have debilitating and life-shortening diseases. On closer inspection, however, each possesses an inner peace and sense of worth for which movie stars, politicians, and wealthy CEOs would trade all their earthly gains. *Personal Values* lays out a blueprint for these true heroes and heroines of our world—those that have come to enjoy that higher plane.

The evidence clearly supports that the game plan laid out in these pages will make you physically, mentally, and spiritually healthier, and allow you to lead a life of significance—the life that God intended you to live. Following God's road map won't necessarily make your life easier or your bank account bigger. There will be times when this framework will lead you to choose a fork in the road of life that will demand self-sacrifice. So it is with those who have been called by God to follow Jesus's footsteps. In the words of Dietrich Bonhoeffer, "To endure the cross is not a tragedy; it is the suffering which is the fruit of an exclusive allegiance to Jesus Christ."[6] If your goal is to add lasting real value to your life, both on this earth and beyond, I urge you to read on.

The Bible provides us with a values system and a way to integrate those values that enable us to serve our coworkers, our neighbors, and our family and, in so doing, serve ourselves. The outcome of living according to these principles is that—by word and deed—we witness to those around us about the life of significance we have in Christ. In other words, we become enabled to fulfill the Great Commission: "Therefore go and make disciples of all nations, baptizing them in the name of the Father and of the Son and of the Holy Spirit, and teaching them to obey everything I have commanded you. And surely I am with you always, to the very end of the age" (Matt. 28:19-20).

Robert Bellah and his colleagues, in their landmark book, *Habits of the Heart,* proposed that Americans do not have a moral framework to make sense of life. They demonstrate how, through our shared vocabulary of individualism, it is difficult to find meaning and a desire to serve others, if you, like most Americans, believe that "in the end you're really alone, and you only have to answer to yourself."[7] We as a society have forgotten the reason why it is in our interests as well as our responsibility to serve our community. Since 1985, when *Habits of the Heart* was published, we have witnessed many changes—primarily our increasing dependence on computers, the Internet, cell phones, instant messaging, video conferencing, just-in-time manufacturing, and twenty-four-hour-a-day markets, all of which have forced us to live life at warp speed in order to survive. Combining such culturally based hyperindividualism with a never-before-imagined frenetic pace has the potential to kill us—physically and spiritually. As Wayne Muller accurately describes:

> A "successful" life has become a violent enterprise. We make war on our own bodies, pushing them beyond their limits; war on our children, because we cannot find enough time to be with them when they are hurt and afraid, and need our company; war on our spirit, because we are too preoccupied to listen to the quiet voices that seek to nourish and refresh us; war on our communities, because we are fearfully protecting what we have, and do not feel safe enough to be kind and generous; war on the earth, because we cannot take the time to place our feet on the ground and allow it to feed us, to taste its blessings and give thanks.[8]

The time has come to return to a life that God has intended for us. *Personal Values* demonstrates that, by emulating and sharing this framework with others, we will be living out the Christian values Jesus taught and that serve our communities and ourselves. By living out of the framework of God's Game Plan for Life, we will be able to take back our life and reconnect with our families and our God. And, along the way, we will rediscover ourselves.

Rabbi Zusya once told his students, "In the next life, I shall not be asked, 'Why were you not Moses or Isaac or Jacob?' I shall be asked: 'Why were you not Zusya?'"[9] God has a plan for each of us. God told the prophet Jeremiah, "Before I formed you in the womb I knew you, before you were born I set you apart; I appointed you as a prophet to the nations" (Jer. 1:5). Likewise, God has also set you and me apart and has a unique plan for each of our lives. *Personal Values* will help each of us be the person God intended us to be, to live the life God intended us to live. It is a game plan to integrate biblical principles into our post-modern lives that will allow us to live a God-pleasing life of significance. It is my prayer that God will not one day have to ask you, "Why were you not who I intended you to be?"

Remember the television commercial in which Victor Kiam, the CEO of Remington electric shavers, tells us that "he liked the product so much that he bought the company." Similarly, I like this game plan so much I had to write the book. I did not intend to write such a personal story, but once I discovered how the journey led me back to a genuine faith—the "hidden secret" of my life—I simply had no choice but to share it with others. For now, this is my calling.

Personal Values—A Journal to Create Your Own Personal Game Plan

The questions at the end of each chapter are designed to help you create your own personal Game Plan for Life. Various quotes and passages are used to stimulate inquiry, discussion, and self-reflection.

I also invite you to share your insights or observations with others by sending them to values@SenskeValues.com. Many of the insights will be posted on www.SenskeValues.com so that others may also benefit from your journey. Please let us know if you would like the response to be confidential, or if we are allowed to use your name. This will allow each of us an opportunity to serve each other, as well as incorporate the knowledge gained from their journey into our own personal journey.

"The Christian life comes not by gritting our teeth but by falling in love."
—Richard Foster

What does this statement mean to you in terms of your relationship with God? How this has influenced the way you live?

Have there been times when you haven't felt this way? What were the consequences?

"All That You Have Is Your Soul"
—Tracy Chapman song title

What implications does this statement have in terms of how we are to live our lives?

"Faith is not belief. Belief is passive. Faith is active."
—Edith Hamilton

Do you agree with this statement? How does your own personal faith play out in your daily life?

"When you live in light of eternity, your values change."
—Rick Warren

What does this statement mean? How has your personal faith changed your values? Is there a correlation between the strength of our relationship with God and our ability to live out our values?

chapter one

God's playbook

I want to know the mind of God—the rest is detail.
—Albert Einstein

As a Christian, I believe that Jesus Christ died and rose for my sins, and that I am saved for eternity. Before I am able to receive this gift I must—as Martin Luther held—completely despair of my own ability before I am prepared to receive the grace of Jesus Christ.[1] I am not saved because of anything I have done or by how successful I am at leading a godly life. It is all because of Jesus. Once we truly comprehend the magnitude of this gift, we become overwhelmed by our desire to worship and serve God. We strive to follow God's commands because this is what God asks us to do. God is indeed merciful and gracious. Through both the Old and New Testaments, God has made it clear that we are to live a meaningful and healthy life during our short stay here on earth.

This is the kind of life that Jesus makes possible. He states, "I have come that they may have life, and have it to the full" (John 10:10). Such fullness is derived from Jesus, the Word made flesh, the One revealed in the Bible as Redeemer. And it is the Scriptures we turn to in order to find direction in daily living. The Bible is our playbook. In the words of John Calvin, "We owe to Scripture the same reverence we owe to God." God's Game Plan for Life comes complete with an instruction guide, accompanied by God's desire for us to live well, to be well, and to die well, and assigns each of us a unique role during our earthly lives.

We modern-day Christians sometimes forget that there is a close connection in the Bible between a life of faith and a life of health. Yahweh, speaking to the Israelites, promises: "If you listen carefully to the voice of the Lord your God and do what is right in his eyes, if you pay attention to his commands and keep all his decrees, I will not bring on you any of the diseases I brought on the Egyptians, for I am the Lord who heals you" (Exod. 15:26). Jesus told the crowds:

> Your eye is the lamp of your body. When your eyes are good your whole body also is full of light. But when they are bad, your body also is full of darkness. See to it, then, that the light within you is not darkness. Therefore, if your whole body is full of light, and no part of it dark, it will be completely lighted, as when the light of a lamp shines on you (Luke 11:34-36).

With the gift of Jesus, God provides the freedom to live a life of faith, health, and significance. God's gift of salvation provides inner peace, security, and joy. Even when we feel our faith is not strong enough to lead a godly life, God's grace forgives, strengthens, and makes us whole—makes us *healthy* physically, mentally, spiritually. As we will explore in chapter 3, there is objective proof that following God's playbook helps us to lead a life of significance.

Mind, Body, and Soul

God perceives us as whole people consisting of mind, body, and soul. Over time, we have lost sight of this inner-connectedness of mind, body, and spirit. The result is a view of medicine that separates what God intended to be one. The physician focuses on our physical health, the pastor on our soul, and the therapist on our emotional well-being. Our culture places a premium on physical beauty and relegates any conversation about our soul to Sunday morning or the Christian aisle at the local bookstore. It is disheartening that we as a society have done a poor job at caring for any of the dimensions of our being, let alone caring for our whole selves.

The statistics demonstrate that, despite the fact that Americans spend more than one trillion dollars on healthcare every year, we are failing miserably in our earthly quest to be healthy—witness the fact that 55 percent of us are overweight, that, even though America is the wealthiest nation in the world, its citizens rank merely twenty-second in longevity, and have some of the highest incidence of heart disease, cancer, stroke, and diabetes in the world. More than fifty million Americans alone suffer from high blood pressure.[2] The late John Knowles, former president of the Rockefeller Foundation, observed, "Over 99 percent of us are born healthy and suffer premature death and disability only as a result of personal misbehavior and environmental conditions."[3]

Our people also suffer emotionally. More than fifty-one million Americans suffer from mental disorders, and seventeen million are seriously depressed. We long for meaning but don't know how to talk to God. In the words of German theologian Michael Utsch, "The maintenance of the relationship between man and God seems to have expired or at least gone stale. One simply has lost the expertise."[4]

Clearly something has gone wrong. We have fragmented the whole person God has created us to be. God did not intend for us to compartmentalize our health; everything we do affects our well-being. As anthropologist Garth Ludwig states, "We are one, whole, and undivided. . . . Each of us is a totality. I do not have a body. I *am* a body. I do not have a mind. I *am* a mind. I do not have a spirit. I *am* a spirit."[5] Similarly, theologian William Watty describes the biblical view of ourselves:

One of the basic concepts of man we have in the Bible is one of totality. Man is a psychosomatic being through and through, with all that this entails. In the story of creation we read that God formed man out of the dust of the ground and breathed into his nostrils the breath *(ruah)* of life and man became a living *nephesh,* which may be translated as "soul." The *nephesh* is not something apart from the body, it is the totality of man, a living soul. It is not that the body has a soul; man is a living soul and it is better to think of him as an animated body, rather than an incarnated soul.[6]

The apostle Paul substantiates this view, "May your whole spirit, soul and body be kept blameless at the coming of our Lord Jesus Christ" (1 Thess. 5:23). Garth Ludwig provides us with the following diagram to illustrate the point:

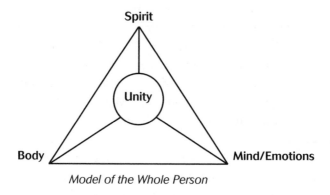

Model of the Whole Person

Elizabeth Skogland, a Christian therapist, also has written about the interdependence of these systems:

> Convenient as it may be to compartmentalize a human being and say: "This problem is all spiritual or all psychological or all physical," such an attitude is simplistic and can increase a person's difficulties. While people are made up of all these components, each interrelates with the other until they often become blurred and indistinguishable one from the other.[7]

As stewards of God's creation, we have a responsibility to care for ourselves in totality. We are called actively to care for our mind, body, and soul. This is the first step in understanding the dynamics of God's Game Plan for Life.

Shalom

My search for creating my own personal Game Plan for Life surprisingly kept bringing me back to the Old Testament. There God first described the interrelationship between our body, mind, and soul. The Jewish community of the Old Testament properly understood that it is not so much that we are to keep the Commandments, as it is that the Commandments keep us. God's game plan is not designed to do us harm; it is intended to keep us healthy in every way. In so doing, we are able to better serve our Creator. For centuries, this understanding has been largely compromised by the subsequent and continuing influence of Greek philosophy and its focus on the separation of the body and soul.[8] Fortunately, new discoveries in medical science are bringing us back to our Old Testament roots.

God's game plan is centered on the concept of *shalom*, which translates as "peace" or "wholeness." Under God's covenant of shalom, God binds us not only to himself, but to each other, as well as to all of creation. John Wilkinson, a British physician, medical missionary, and biblical scholar, states in *The Bible and Healing*, "Human wholeness or health is the main topic of the Bible. . . . It is only when human beings are whole and their relationships right, that they can be described as truly healthy."[9] Walt Larrimore further describes how in the ancient Hebrew Scriptures the root word *rapha*, which describes the process of healing, is used eighty-six times. The variety of uses for *rapha* demonstrates that healing is not only limited to the physical realm. God desires that healing for every aspect of our life be restored—physical, mental, social, and spiritual.[10] Larimore correctly asserts, "Our overall health depends not just on our physical health, important as that is, but also on our inner life. It is this emotional and spiritual life that God most wants to nourish and promote, for he knows that without spiritual and emotional well-being, we are less healthy than we were designed to be."[11]

Biblical scholar Walter Brueggemann describes three aspects of shalom. First, shalom represents God's power to bring harmony to our world. Without shalom, the earth was "formless and empty, darkness was over the surface of the deep" (Gen. 1:2). With shalom disorder is turned "into harmony—so that light, life, joy become possible."[12] As Paul writes about Jesus in Colossians 1:17, "He is before all things, and in him all things hold together."

It is the next two aspects of shalom Brueggemann identified that are most relevant for purposes of developing our own individual game plan. The second realm of shalom centers around the principles of justice and righteousness. The Old Testament prophets describe how the absence of shalom results in social disorder.

The prophet Micah:

Woe to those who plan iniquity
to those who plot evil on their beds! . . .
They covet fields and seize them,
And houses and take them.
They defraud a man of his home,
a fellowman of his inheritance (2:1-2).

The prophet Amos:

Hear this word you cows of Bashan on Mount Samaria,
you women who oppress the poor and crush the needy
and say to your husbands, "Bring us some drinks!" (4:1).

Seek good, not evil,
that you may live. . . .

Hate evil, love good;
maintain justice in the courts (5:14-15).

The prophet Isaiah:

Wash and make yourselves clean.
Take your evil deeds
out of my sight!
Stop doing wrong,
learn to do right!
Seek justice,
encourage the oppressed.
Defend the cause of the fatherless,
plead the case of the widow (1:16-17).

King David:

Turn from evil and do good;
seek peace and pursue it (Ps. 34:14).

Brueggemann explains, "The consequence of justice and righteousness is shalom—an enduring sabbath of joy and well-being." Brueggemann extends this analysis to the New Testament as well. "Jesus's ministry to the excluded (see Luke 4:16-21) was the same, the establishment of community between those who were excluded and those who had excluded them. His acts of healing the sick, forgiving the guilty, raising the dead, and feeding the hungry are all actions of reestablishing God's will for shalom in a world gone chaotic by callous self-seeking."[13]

Bringing justice and righteousness into our world can be accomplished only if we turn from being a self-centered, inward-focused sinner to an other-centered, outward-focused disciple. This leads us to the third aspect of shalom, which provides the cornerstone for God's Game Plan for Life. It contrasts the sense of well-being that is experienced by a person who lives a life of shalom, a "caring, sharing, joyous life in community" versus living a life of self-centeredness and mindless pursuit of possession.[14] The prophets as well as Jesus compare a life of shalom versus this self-centered way of living. God, speaking through Isaiah, states in no uncertain terms:

> "I was enraged by his sinful greed;
> I punished him, and hid my face in anger,
> yet he kept on his willful ways.
> Peace, peace [shalom] to those far and near,"
> says the Lord. "And I will heal them."
> But the wicked are like the tossing sea,
> which cannot rest,
> whose waves cast up mire and mud.
> "There is no peace [shalom], says my God, for the wicked"
> (Isa. 57:17, 19-21).

And, in Luke's gospel, a man comes to Jesus and says,

> "Teacher, tell my brother to divide the inheritance with me." . . .
> Then [Jesus] said to them, "Watch out! Be on your guard against all kinds of greed; a man's life does not consist in the abundance of his possessions. . . . Therefore I tell you, do not worry about your life, what you will eat; or about your body, what you will wear" (12:13, 15, 22).

What the Bible clearly rejects is a lifestyle that seeks security and pleasure at the expense of others or at the expense of God's creation. We begin to know shalom only by participating in God's community, by taking care of other people and God's creation. Paul puts it most succinctly when he tells us simply that Jesus himself is our shalom (Eph. 2:14).[15] And although sin prevents each of us from achieving perfect wholeness during our brief earthly stay, God's promise to us is that at the end of the age,

Jesus will return to complete and perfect the healing process (Mal. 4:2; Rev. 22:2).

Relating Shalom to Our Own Lives

God is our healer. "I am the Lord who heals you" (Exod. 15:26). God provides significance, health, and salvation through shalom—through the command that we serve others. Under God's Game Plan for Life, we win by being other-directed. Garth Ludwig, in his seminal book, *Order Restored: A Biblical Interpretation of Health, Medicine, and Healing*, describes the Old Testament concept of shalom:

> Throughout the Old Testament shalom has the meaning of "well-being" in the widest sense of that word and encompasses prosperity (Ps. 73:3), bodily health (Isa. 57:18, Ps. 38:3), and also salvation (Isa. 43:7). . . .
>
> Health for the Hebrews was more than a state of physical and psychological wellness as the Western world usually defines that term. Health was rather received as a state of "wholeness" that assumed the unity of all things under the rule of God. In the Hebrew world view, health included a person's relationship to God as well as his relationship to his family, community, livestock, and even his property. It assumes the integration of all dimensions of life as well as the universe in which one lives; an imbalance in one part adversely affects the other parts.[16]

William Watty further describes the Hebrews' conception of shalom:

> Health was not considered something physical, but total. In the 23rd Psalm, Yahweh restores my nephesh, which means not only spiritual refreshment, but also physical recovery and social rehabilitation. The word for health in Hebrew is shalom

and the word is the same for "peace," "welfare," "well-being," and "harmony." Health is total. It is personal well-being. It is social harmony and justice. It is walking humbly with God.[17]

Ludwig comments that the key to living this balanced life of health and significance is twofold: (1) Developing our personal relationship with God; and (2) Reflecting the nature of God in every dimension of our existence—physical, social, and spiritual.[18] As Ludwig describes, "Health is the *wholeness* of God's creative love at work in our lives. It is the expression of what God has created us to be—functionally, mentally, emotionally, socially, and spiritually."[19] Jesus promises us the blessing of shalom: "I have come that they may have life, and have it to the full" (John 10:10). In fact, true wholeness is impossible apart from Christ. Abigail Rian Evans of Princeton Theological Seminary notes, "To see the link between salvation and healing is to recognize the full sense of wholeness."[20] What is exciting is that if we live out our personal values and develop a closer relationship with God daily, you and I are able to link our everyday actions to our multifaceted health and feel the wholeness in our lives that God so intently wants us to achieve.

Because of our sinful nature we are constantly at war with ourselves. We seek that which pleases us and takes care of our short-term needs and desires. We go through the day bombarded by temptations and often compromise our faith to fit within the ways of the world. Despite our desire to serve God and others, we often don't succeed. Abigail Rian Evans describes the tension within ourselves:

> The body identifies us with basic animal impulses, but also serves as the "temple of the Holy Spirit." The mind centers both instinct and impulse and reflective and creative powers. Mental states may predispose persons to illness as well as release vital forces in preventing sickness. The spirit enables us to transcend ourselves and our world.[21]

Living a life of shalom is God's solution to winning the war against this sin-caused tension in our lives.

Achieving Wholeness

God's Game Plan for Life is the path that leads us to wholeness. Because of our sinful nature, you and I will never achieve complete wholeness during our earthly lives. That will only occur on the day of resurrection. On this day shalom will be complete and we will experience the fullness of God's kingdom.[22] Nowhere does the Bible guarantee that if we follow God's path of wholeness, perfect physical, mental, or spiritual health follow automatically. The powers of Satan, although defeated, continue to do battle with us. We live in a broken world where illness and disease are but one consequence. Sin and sickness are connected although not necessarily in a causal way. Rather, when we become sick or disabled it is a sign that we belong to a state of fallen humanity.[23] Ludwig also provides a second explanation for disease and sickness in the Old Testament: one of discipline and correction. Job hears this as advice from a friend: "Blessed is the man whom God corrects; so do not despise the discipline of the Almighty. For he wounds, but he also binds up; he injures, but his hands also heal" (Job 5:17-18). Although we will never fully understand God's ways this side of heaven, it is clear throughout the Old Testament that the Lord alone has the power to heal and grant salvation.[24]

This absence of a causal connection is again emphasized in the New Testament when the disciples inquired of Jesus, "Rabbi, who sinned, this man or his parents, that he was born blind?" (John 9:2). Jesus responded, "Neither this man nor his parents sinned, but this happened so that the work of God might be displayed in his life." Martin Scharlemann correctly states that "health is only a *penultimate*, a next-to-the-last gift and not the ultimate reality."[25] As described in the Lutheran Confessions, our earthly troubles are "works of God, intended for our profit, that the power of God might be made more manifest in our weakness."[26]

In describing why Jesus didn't heal the entire world, Scharlemann goes on to explain:

> Jesus did not engage in such universal healing by divine fiat for the same reason that He did not jump from the pinnacle of the temple. He did not come to gather followers in any other way than by asking them to see in His work a token of that full restoration which God had in mind for all his faithful ones at the end of history.[27]

We never reach a complete state of shalom or wholeness. We are engaged in a process just as life is a process. As human beings we continually strive to better ourselves and search for new answers. Abigail Rian Evans, in her book, *Redeeming Marketplace Medicine: A Theology of Health Care,* talks about attaining wholeness: "From a theological perspective, health is an eschatological idea, that is, what God promises and offers in the end. We do not know completely what health is because we have not totally enjoyed it."[28] Another way of looking at health is that those of us who enjoy good health (by earthly standards) can take advantage of this blessing and focus on strengthening our spiritual and mental spheres by using our God-given physical attributes to serve others.

Likewise, those of us who suffer a debilitating disease, a physical handicap or mental limitation can indeed also experience the wholeness of health. Within this framework we are not measured by earthly standards, but rather by heavenly standards. God measures our health by our ability to live a life of wholeness, a life of shalom. What results is an exhilarating freedom that this new model provides us. No longer do we measure ourselves by the false, impossible-to-achieve standards created by Madison Avenue—the perfect bodies, endless supply of toys, chasing of new experiences in order to feel alive. Rather, we measure ourselves by the framework that our compassionate and loving God has provided us, which teaches us to lead a life of significance and wholeness. As Ludwig notes, "Yet even now, although disease and suffering remain, the blessings of wholeness in the kingdom of God are freely available to all."[29]

God may even use sickness and disease as a tool to bring us closer to God or to add a new dimension of wholeness to our life. Accomplishing God's Game Plan for Life includes taking into account our chronic pain, disabilities, sickness, chemical imbalances, and weaknesses. Those that have life-limiting illnesses often do much better than those of us who are healthy in understanding what is important in life and what is trivial and meaningless. In *The Wounded Healer*, Henri Nouwen describes it this way:

> A Christian community is a healing community not because wounds are cured and pains are alleviated, but because wounds and pains become openings or occasions for a new vision. Mutual confession then becomes a mutual deepening of hope, and sharing weakness becomes a reminder to one and all of the coming strength.[30]

Rev. John Bade is a friend and colleague. In 1989, at the age of thirty-one, while serving as a pastor in Austin, Texas, John was diagnosed with Parkinson's disease. He recently wrote a moving poetic journal of his fourteen-year struggle with this debilitating disease titled, *Will I Sing Again?* In this insightful book Bade honestly describes his ensuing tortuous journey full of pain, stress, weariness, anxiety, fear, anger, depression, and hope. When asked why he was struck with Parkinson's, Bade bravely replies:

> For these many years,
> I have always answered the question
> by pointing to the hidden blessing.
> "Perhaps God has used the Parkinson's"
> I say courageously,
> "to enhance my ministry.

As I share my weakness and my struggle,
I allow others to share their struggle.
I give voice and words to the grief."
It was the best—the only—answer I could with integrity give
to this unexplained suffering and affliction,
this thorn of the flesh.

At times, I want to curse the All-Powerful God
who allows illness, sorrow, and loss to exist.

But then I see the cross;
and I begin to truly see.

Upon this thorn
has become a beautiful rose—
a rich, fragrant flower painted in word and verse.

I realize now
that this rose would not have come to bud
save for the thorn;
and the beauty and glory of this precious flower
could have not blossomed
were it not for the watering of the tears
from the pain of the suffering and affliction.

And once more,
the cross becomes the crown
the thorns becomes the flower
and the curse becomes the blessing
in the powerful, creative hands of God.[31]

Like the death of Jesus on the cross, what appears to be a horrific tragedy is in reality the greatest good, eternal life.[32] The Christian perspective is that sickness, chronic disease, suffering, and even death are in fact positive events in our lives that provide opportunities for spiritual and personal growth as well as eternal life. It is part of what Christians describe as "the theology of the cross," the key to living a life of wholeness.

Dying Well
In our health-crazed, consumer-driven, capitalist society we shun the dying, pretend they no longer exist and secretly hope that they "go soon." We all hope and pray that personally we live a long and healthy life and then quickly die. Keith Meador, the director of the Duke University Institute on Care at the End of Life, looks differently at dying well.

> Historically, dying well would have been understood in the Christian community as the opportunity to be at peace with God and one's neighbors prior to dying. The vision was that if one were blessed with the opportunity to know of one's impending death and be able to accomplish those goals at the end of life, it was considered a good death.
>
> We have lost that vision in contemporary culture. Within modernity, the assumption is that to die quickly and painlessly is the priority. I think meeting the needs of adequate pain management is important but more important is allowing people to have time to do the work of living that comes at the end of life.[33]

Meador urges us to embrace the dying rather than avoid them in order to learn from their struggles. He goes on to note that an awareness of our own vulnerability is healthy in allowing us to separate the important from the trivial in our lives.[34] For Christians, death itself is healing. Under God's Game Plan for Life we are allowed to embrace our own vulnerabilities and inevitable death, which paradoxically allows us to live life to its fullest.

What Next?
Garth Ludwig reminds us that, "In actuality all of life is a movement towards death."[35] Acknowledging this fact allows us to

incorporate God's Game Plan for Life into all of our daily living. If we are open and willing, our daily march to death is an opportunity for us to be transformed. Through our brokenness and our intentional relationship with the Holy Spirit we catch an occasional glimpse of God and experience a greater understanding of the wholeness that awaits us. The question becomes: How do we transcend our self-centered ways and narcissistic world in which we live in order to attain the wholeness that God promises? How do we incorporate the biblical concept of shalom into our complex twenty-first-century lives? God's Game Plan for Life provides us with five plays that provide us with the winning strategy. The next chapter will outline the five plays that each of us must implement within our own lives in order to achieve shalom or wholeness.

Journal Questions—God's Playbook

"I intend to live forever—so far, so good."
   —Comedian, Steven Wright

How does the concept of shalom affect our understanding of this line?

"The greatest error in the treatment of the human body is that physicians are ignorant of the whole. For the part can never be well unless the whole is well."
   —Plato

Provide an example from your own personal life when an imbalance in your physical, mental, or spiritual sphere led to suffering in another sphere.

"We learn truth in proportion to our suffering."
—Søren Kierkegaard

How has a physical or mental ailment, tragic loss, or difficult situation brought you closer to God? How has it allowed you to realize what is truly important in life?

"Wholeness or well-being is not the absence of brokenness. Instead it is what you choose, at the center of your life, to do with your brokenness."
—Howard Clinebell

What brokenness in your life comes to mind? What have you done with this brokenness? What else can you do to use this brokenness to your advantage in your quest to become whole?

"The Lord confides in those who fear him; he makes his covenant known to them."
—Psalm 25:14

What does the psalmist mean by "those who fear him"? In what way should you and I fear God? Does fearing our Lord allow us to more effectively embrace a life of shalom?

the five plays

There is a wonderful mythical law of nature that the three things we crave most in life—happiness, freedom, and peace of mind—are always attained by giving them to someone else.
—Peyton Conway March

Many of us, despite our many differences, share the same goals:

- A loving family (where members actually like each other)
- A life of balance and significance
- Great health—physically, mentally, and spiritually
- A close relationship with God

By following God's Game Plan for Life we move toward accomplishing these goals. The plan, simply put, is a framework for living out our values through a life of significance by serving others, which, in turn, benefits us. In doing so, we reflect the image of God.

To be sure, there is more than one way a person can apply the shalom of God to their life. I offer the following Five Plays as a strategy that has worked well for me, in the hope that you might find it "life-giving." These plays comprise our playbook—our framework for living. As players on God's team, together we strive to execute these plays well, and it is teamwork that allows us—individually and collectively—to live a life of wholeness and significance.

Play 1—Take Care of Yourself

The first play in our playbook is to focus on our own personal health. Paul instructs us, "Do you not know that your body is a temple of the Holy Spirit, who is in you, whom you have received from God? You are not your own; you were bought at a price. Therefore honor God with your body" (1 Cor. 6:19-20). G. Lloyd Rediger, pastoral counselor and author, describes caring for our mind, body, and soul as a reflection of our salvation; it is a God-directed process of self-management, good stewardship of our personhood, resources, and environment, and a significant aspect of our proclamation of the gospel.[1] A key aspect of honoring God requires that we focus on becoming healthy in every facet of our being. Rediger explains, "There is no condition as being fit only in spirit or mind or body. All three support each other's shared fitness or suffer from each other's sickness."[2] He cites Adam and Eve as the first examples of the monumental consequences of mental and spiritual unfitness.[3]

Our modern definitions of health tend to be "I" oriented. How do I feel? How do I look? How do I remain young? Am I at peace with the world? How do I achieve a heightened state of awareness? At the same time, we abuse our health by our indulgent and excessive lifestyles, poor exercise and eating habits, and an undisciplined spiritual life. These destructive behaviors are the result of an imbalance in what God intended to be harmonious. We cannot be physically healthy if we aren't spiritually and mentally fit. Similarly, our mental health suffers if we aren't physically and spiritually healthy. A physically fit body builder may suffer from a malnourished mental and spiritual life. A church worker's spiritual life may suffer if she is physically unfit.

I am not talking about achieving perfection; however, each of us is responsible to care for every aspect of ourselves. Such self-care is the work of God. By it, we see more clearly the path God desires us to walk. And that journey calls us to care for others in their totality. The integration of our mind, body, and spirit is at the core of living a life of significance. The key to enriching our health comes from God's word, which strengthens our relationships of faith at home, at work, at church, and in the community.

The pursuit of health should never become an end in itself. Garth Ludwig comments, "If an individual has made health the supreme goal of his life, the *'summum bonum'* of human existence, then health has become an idol of his own making. . . . What is the point of wellness if it has no God-ordained purpose?"[4] The fact is (and the research supports) that if we attend solely to our physical well-being, we will never become truly healthy. Neither can a person who devotes his life to serving the needs of others at the expense of his physical or spiritual health, become a whole person. Under God's Game Plan for Life, our goal is to attain balance between all three spheres.

Play 2—Care for the Environment

Wholeness demands that we think beyond ourselves; we must also consider the needs of others, and we must be concerned about our earth. Shalom encompasses both inner unity and outer social harmony.[5] Ludwig provides us with a drawing of the biblical model of health:

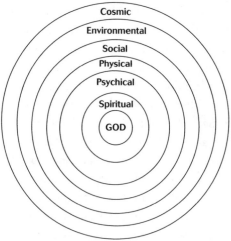

The Biblical Model of Health

As illustrated, there is a direct correlation between personal health and global responsibility. Where I live in Austin, Texas, there are designated "ozone action days" on which people with respiratory problems are warned not to go outside. In the spring the sky over the city is filled with smoke that has drifted northward from Mexico, where the annual burning of fields takes place. On a global level, acid rain, disappearing rainforests, polluted bodies of water, and depleted resources all contribute to a planet that is becoming unable to support itself and its inhabitants. Since 1950 we have lost 20 percent of the earth's topsoil. A cartoon in the *Washington Post* pictures a couple at the breakfast table, the husband is reading a newspaper. His wife looks at him and asks, "So, outside of the people, water, air, and land, how's this world doing?" He had no answer.

God commanded Adam to care for the garden God had made (Gen. 2:15). We, too, who live in God's wonderful garden we call earth, are called to be good gardeners. Shalom includes rediscovering how to live within our ecological constraints. We must recognize that the environment isn't just a political issue; it is a universal issue that plays a vital role in personal wholeness. You and I make decisions every day that improve or harm the environment. They are as simple as deciding whether to recycle our cans, as controversial as whether or not to buy a gas-guzzling SUV, as complex as spending resources to tighten pollution standards in developing countries. The myriad decisions we make, as individuals or as a society, will determine the extent to which we are able to become whole while living on this earth.

Play 3—Serve Others

As Rick Warren so aptly describes in *The Purpose-Driven Life: What on Earth Am I Here For?*[6] living a life of service isn't only a strategy to live well that we have initiated. It is the natural outcome of our relationship with God. We were created to serve God. "For we are God's workmanship, created in Christ Jesus to do good works, which God has prepared in advance for us to do" (Eph. 2:10). We were saved to serve God. "You were bought at a price. Therefore honor God with your body" (1 Cor. 6:20). We are called to serve God. "Who has saved us and called us to a holy life—not because of anything we have done but because of his own purpose and grace" (2 Tim. 1:9). We are commanded to serve God. "[A]nd whoever wants to be first must be your slave—just as the Son of Man did not come to be served, but to serve, and to give his life as a ransom for many" (Matt. 20:27-28).

Paul in his letter to the Romans, exhorts his followers to live lives of service:

> Therefore, I urge you, brothers, in view of God's mercy, to offer your bodies as living sacrifices, holy and pleasing to God—this is your spiritual act of worship. Do not conform any longer to the pattern of this world, but be transformed by the renewing of your mind. Then you will be able to test and approve what God's will is—his good, pleasing and perfect will (Rom. 12:1-2).

Part of shalom is broadening our understanding of wholeness to include caring about the health of others. As we will see in the next chapter, research reflects the fact that our individual health and that of others are interwoven. In serving others we enhance our personal health; in the process of attaining personal harmony, we serve others. As Abigail Rian Evans describes, "One only is whole who is joined to the suffering of others. In other words, one cannot be in full health without sharing the burdens of others' sickness. Wholeness is not solely an individual achievement but, in part, a joint adventure."[7]

We have all experienced the inner satisfaction of helping another—our children, a coworker, or a friend. Some refer to this as a "helper's high," part and parcel of shalom. Living within the kingdom of God is living a life of significance, one that involves the responsibility and privilege of caring for others. Ludwig refers to this as living out our "story." The story in a mother's life might be her journey of caring for her family, working part-time to make ends meet, buying groceries for the elderly neighbor next door, and volunteering at her local church. In so doing, she lives out "the love of Christ who has brought wholeness to her life."[8] Through the presence of the Holy Spirit, by prayer and discernment, we discover our own story. By living out our story we catch a glimpse of wholeness and of God.

The word *wholeness* is related to *holistic*—or *wholistic*—health. Biologist and explorer Jan Smuts introduced this concept by describing nature's tendency to synthesize and organize toward greater wholes.[9] Dennis Jaffe further explains this theory: "The meaning of the whole organism was always more than merely the sum of the parts, because the merging process itself contained certain properties within it." Each of us can properly be understood only within the total functioning of mind, body, and soul.[10] When all are in harmony (the goal of the Game Plan for Life), the result is greater than the individual parts. Each impacts the other: when I help another, not only do I benefit, so does that person, as well as the global community. This is God's strange albeit wonderful math, where one plus one equals three.

Play 4—Let the Holy Spirit Empower You

True peace is the product of the Holy Spirit living within us. Lloyd Rediger points out that spiritual healing is the context for all other healing.[11] Lack of spiritual health results in destructive behavior, excess consumerism, and insecurity—all of which directly affects one's mental and physical health. J. Heinrich Arnold of the Bruderhof community recalled that his father used to tell him that stupidity is the greatest sin. "He did not mean simplicity of mind, but spiritual dullness: having a dead conscience and not listening in one's heart to God."[12]

For many of us, including myself, the most difficult dimension of wholeness is the spiritual dimension. Unlike my physical or intellectual attributes, the health of my soul cannot be measured. It is nebulous, difficult to describe. I cannot determine whether the "good feeling" I have on a particular day at the beach is the work of the Holy Spirit, or the natural consequence of the beauty that surrounds me. For years I didn't feel that the Holy Spirit was "within me." I wasn't even sure what that phrase meant. I doubted the strength and validity of my Christian faith. What I had failed to realize was that, by God's grace, the Spirit was already in my heart, whether or not I "felt" that presence. In my Lutheran tradition, the Spirit's presence is a gift of my baptism. It is the power of the Holy Spirit that enables me to live the life God intends for me to live. I can, however, quench the Spirit's work in my life through selfishness and an unwillingness to serve others. Conversely, I can cooperate with the Holy Spirit in a life of service.

One simply cannot be whole without possessing a healthy soul. Garth Ludwig states:

> The life of the spirit is the foundation stone of our human identity and integrates all other aspects of our personhood in the purposiveness of living. If the spirit is alienated from God, this is bound to have consequences in a person's character as well as in a person's health. Jesus confirmed the truth of this process when he said, "If then the light within you is darkness, how great is that darkness!" (Matt. 6:23)[13]

We learn from the Bible of the presence of the Holy Spirit within us as a gift of God's grace, and such presence compels and enables us toward a life of selflessness and charity toward others.

By nature we are egotistical and self-centered. Living amid material comfort and earthly success, we place the Holy Spirit on the backburner, and ourselves on the front. In so doing, faith becomes merely a function—a duty to think about on Sunday morning. This path leads to smug self-righteousness. But the Bible teaches that the Holy Spirit works through a broken, humble heart. In the Gospel of Matthew the Spirit is compared to a dove (3:16). J. Heinrich Arnold explains this significance:

> A dove is gentle; it will harm no one, and it will not force itself on anyone. It flees before birds of prey. Through the fall of man we are all birds of prey, and we have all driven the Holy Spirit away without knowing it. If the Spirit is resisted, he disappears. He comes only to the lowly, the broken, and those who seek him.[14]

Considering all this, then, it would be more accurate to say that God is the Playmaker for Play 4. In the broadest sense, God is the motivating force behind our every intention in God's Game Plan for Life, but it is the stirring of the Holy Spirit within us that is the basis for all other "plays." From there, the movement is always outward. Arnold says, "The experience of the Holy Spirit can never remain an individual experience: it leads to community."[15] Using our language, this experience points us toward wholeness. Life in the Spirit means continually approaching God as a humble sinner, asking forgiveness when we fail. George P. Vanier, former governor-general of Canada, kept these thoughts by his bedside:

> There is no use arguing about it, you are going to be asked to give daily to a combination of these three exercises: prayer, reflection, and spiritual reading. No matter how busy you are, no man is too busy to eat; neither is any man too busy to feed his soul. And if we starve our souls, we will deprive our lives, busy though they may be, of their fruitfulness.[16]

In my personal journey I have become more attuned to the role of the Holy Spirit through Bible study, prayer, and contemplation. I value these more than the many books I have read; I have come to understand that "heart" knowledge surpasses "head" knowledge. John Michael Talbot, describing the life of St. Francis of Assisi, says that, "Francis' goal in life wasn't to be Italy's most respected religious scholar. . . . He wanted to be deeply and madly in love with God." Talbot explains: "[T]he world is full of people who mistake knowing things about God for actually knowing God."[17] Over the twenty years of my quest, I had learned much about God, but did not feel I knew God. Knowing God has made me more aware of the Spirit's joyous presence.

The apostle Paul is one of my heroes. Before his Damascus road conversion, he persecuted the followers of Jesus. After his conversion, he served Jesus admirably, despite physical illness, imprisonment, hardships, torture, and strife. He sometimes fought with colleagues, admitted his weaknesses, and often questioned his worth. In other words, he was a lot like you and me. He reveals much about his personal struggle in the seventh chapter of Romans, where he confessed that he cannot do anything right. He considers himself an utter failure at trying to live up to God's standards. His tension is unbearable:

> We know that the law is spiritual; but I am unspiritual, sold as a slave to sin. I do not understand what I do. For what I want to do I do not do, but what I hate I do. . . . For I have the desire to do what is good, but I cannot carry it out. For what I do is not the good I want to do; no, the evil I do not want to do—this I keep on doing. . . . What a wretched man I am (Rom. 7:14-15, 18-19, 24)!

At the point of despair, Paul focuses on himself, using the word *I* thirty times in this chapter. But he declares the solution as coming from outside himself, "Thanks be to God—through Jesus Christ our Lord!" Paul weaves in the vital role of the Holy Spirit in living a life of significance.

> Those who live according to the sinful nature have their minds set on what that nature desires; but those who live in accordance with the Spirit have their minds set on what the Spirit

desires. The mind of sinful man is death, but the mind controlled by the Spirit is life and peace (Rom. 8:5-6).

We do not know what we ought to pray, but the Spirit himself intercedes for us with groans that words cannot express. And he who searches our hearts knows the mind of the Spirit, because the Spirit intercedes for the saints in accordance with God's will (Rom. 8:26-27).

How do you know whether the Holy Spirit lives within you? First and foremost, because God promises it. In his sermon on the day of Pentecost, Peter told the crowd, "Repent and be baptized, every one of you, in the name of Jesus Christ so that your sins may be forgiven. And you will receive the gift of the Holy Spirit" (Acts 2:38). Furthermore, the Bible indicates that the Holy Spirit is active in our lives. In the beatitudes Jesus paints a picture of what being a person of God looks like. "[T]hey are meek, they hunger and thirst for righteousness, they are merciful and pure of heart, they are peacemakers, and they are persecuted for righteousness' sake."[18] The apostle Paul writes that the fruits of the presence of the Holy Spirit are love, joy, peace, patience, kindness, goodness, faithfulness, gentleness, and self-control (Gal. 5:22-23). The presence of the Holy Spirit is affirmed in prayer, in service, and in the study of God's word. I must be careful not to quench that work, but to stay true to my constant quest for a life of service.

Play 5—Become Friends with God

Over the years I have learned that prayer is not about asking God to give me what I want—that new job, sinking a putt on the golf course, better investment returns, a life of ease. Rather, prayer is surrendering my own needs so that I can become an instrument of God's work. I begin each day by asking, "God, how can I serve you today?" I then spend the rest of the day "listening" for God's answer even as I go about caring for myself and serving others.

On one level prayer is pretty scary stuff. What if God needs me to serve in Ethiopia, Guatemala, or even North Dakota? What if God needs me to abandon that well-paying job for a calling at much lower pay? On another level, serving God in this way is truly exciting and liberating. I don't have to worry about how I will survive. If God cares enough about the plight of the sparrows or whether a hair has fallen from my head (Matt. 10:29-30), God will certainly care for my financial needs. If I am able to enjoy a successful career early on in life unaware and unappreciative of God's active presence (as I had for years), then surely recognizing it will result in greater fulfillment.

Serving God takes work. I have learned that the more effectively I implement God's Game Plan for Life into my own life, the more my eyes are opened to God's working—doors are opened, contacts are made, opportunities are uncovered. The reward in my Christian walk is the joy of knowing a vibrant relationship with God, and a sense of peace that transcends all understanding (Phil. 4:7). The more fully I live toward wholeness—or, in our language, God's Game Plan for Life—the more clearly I can ascertain God's answer to my prayers. What results is a sense of peace, a sense of shalom. It is the peace that comes from knowing that I am accomplishing what God intends.

Developing our faith is both an individual and communal effort. Mine has been touched by my daughter's childlike faith and my wife's unwavering faith. My coworkers have supported me in my journey; I humbly thank Cecilia, David, Mel, Sam, Regina, Jack, Sherry, Katherine, Mark, Dan, Karen, Keith, and many others. In conversation and by example, they have been an invaluable spiritual resource for me. Whether it is through our congregation's weekly small groups, encounters with friends, or conversations in Christian chat rooms, we can support each other's faith journey, and, at the same time witness to the unchurched. Through God's brilliant design, our desire to strengthen the faith of those around us will, in turn, strengthen our own.

Got Game?

Living a life of shalom does not mean a life of leisure, but rather a life full of challenges and risks. As in the hymn, "Onward, Christian Soldiers," people march to the drumbeat of our Lord and Savior Jesus Christ, and by him are emboldened to face dangers along the way. Ludwig notes, "Paradoxically, being 'healthy' in the biblical perspective may add suffering to our lives."[19] John Sanford adds:

> Becoming whole does not mean being perfect, but being completed. It does not necessarily mean happiness, but growth. It is often painful, but, fortunately, never boring. It is not getting out of life what we think we want, but it is the development and purification of the soul.[20]

To accomplish our goals, we have no choice but to "get in the game" of a life of discipleship. John Sanford rightly comments, "If we stand on the sidelines of life, wholeness cannot emerge."[21]

Wholeness manifests itself in us through the balance of our mind, body, and spirit into a life of service. This melding can be compared to a family farm, where members viewed life in totality, like a meaningful work of art. When someone in the community needs help, you stop what you are doing and help them; when someone needs food, you give them a chicken and vegetables from your garden; when it's harvest time, you work past sunset to help your neighbor get the job done. The words of the apostle Paul to the church in Colosse become our motto, "Whatever you do, work at it with all your heart, as working for the Lord, not for men" (Col. 3:23).

In the process of living our lives in this way, we break down the barriers we erected in splitting the facets of our life. We understand the interconnectedness between our own life, our environment, and the lives of others. We understand how our physical, mental, and spiritual spheres interweave to maintain this fragile balance of our health. Our lives become a God-pleasing work of art and we, as the artists, become part of a dynamic artistic community.

There Are No Injury Time Outs or Age Limitations

A life of service—a life of significance—is our goal, and nothing should dissuade from this path—not poor health, not what we perceive as a lack of special talents, not old age nor any other reason. Rick Warren, in *The Purpose-Driven Life,* states it well:

> If you are not involved in any service or ministry, what excuse have you been using? Abraham was old, Jacob was insecure, Leah was unattractive, Joseph was abused, Moses stuttered, Gideon was poor, Samson was codependent, Rahab was immoral, David had an affair and all kinds of family problems, Elijah was suicidal, Jeremiah was depressed, Jonah was reluctant, Naomi was a widow, John the Baptist was eccentric to say the least, Peter was impulsive and hot-tempered, Martha worried a lot, the Samaritan woman had several failed marriages, Zacchaeus was unpopular, Thomas had doubts, Paul had poor health, and Timothy was timid.[22]

Despite the toll that Parkinson's disease has taken on John Bade, he continually searches for ways to serve. Bade writes:

> By faith . . . I trust that God has something else in store for me. Maybe it's writing a devotional book for those struggling with chronic illness. Maybe it's being the voice for those whose physical voices have been silenced and whose hands have been stilled by diseases such as Parkinson's. Maybe it's helping a congregation as an interim pastor through the tough transition we are facing of saying good-bye to a pastor. Maybe it's serving churches struggling with conflicts to help bring healing. Maybe it's teaching . . . or preaching . . . *or* counseling.[23]

The Five Plays we have outlined form our strategy for following God's Game Plan for Life. God promises to lead us down the path to an eternal life of shalom. Thus enabled by God's grace we are compelled to embark on the journey. We trust intuitively God's promise that there exists an intricate balance between shalom and the state of our physical, mental, and spiritual health. But we can also measure this connection empirically. We will explore this in the next chapter.

Journal Questions—The Five Plays

"Only he who believes is obedient; only he who is obedient believes."
   —Dietrich Bonhoeffer

What ramifications does this statement have in how we lead our own life? How does this idea relate to the Five Plays?

"I thought, 'Age should speak; advanced years should teach wisdom.' But it is the spirit in a man, the breath of the Almighty, that gives him understanding."
   —Job 32:7-8

How does the Holy Spirit work within our life? Why is it so vital that we strengthen our relationship with God?

"God does not work in all hearts alike but according to the preparation and sensitivity he finds in each."
   —Meister Eckhart

How do you prepare your own heart to allow the Holy Spirit to enter in?

"We are greatest when we stoop to serve; we are tallest when we kneel to pray."
   —Gilbert Keith Chesterton

Explain this seeming paradox by providing examples from your own life. What additional opportunities are there for you to become even greater and taller?

"The meaning of earthly existence lies, not as we have grown used to thinking, in prospering, but in the development of the soul."
—Alexandr Solzhenitsyn

Explain the significance of this statement in the context of our complex twenty-first-century lives.

chapter three

the evidence supports the game plan

It is one of the most beautiful compensations of this life that no man can sincerely try to help one another without helping himself.
—Ralph Waldo Emerson

The skeptic inside of us occasionally questions whether something that was written thousands of years ago can still be relevant in our post-modern lives. The prophets surely could not have imagined a world made up of the likes of rappers, AIDS, suicide bombers, nanotechnology, chat rooms, cloning, Amazon.com, and gene therapy. But God's word is timeless, and God's instructions for living are as relevant today as they were in the days of Moses.

This chapter provides an overview of the wide range of research that corroborates God's Game Plan for Life. The research was conducted by those affiliated and unaffiliated with the church. I do not intend to prove God exists, nor is it to convince you to do God's will because it is "good for you," nor to give you a self-help guide to happiness. Rather, I intend to lay before you the scientific evidence that demonstrates that God's Game Plan for Life provides us with a framework for living that brings wholeness to our body, mind, and soul. The research has confirmed for me the veracity of the promise that God is gracious and loving, who wants us to enjoy life to the fullest. God presents us with a strategy for living that is characterized by caring for God's kingdom and God's people. All of this has illuminated my understanding of God's plan, strengthened my faith and my desire to serve God. This broad-based research from a variety of disciplines supports our thesis that living a life according to God's plan is the best path to health, happiness, and significance.

Believing in God Makes for Better Health

The *Handbook of Religion and Health* documents more than sixteen hundred studies and medical review articles exploring the connection between religious belief and activities with emotional, social, and physical health outcomes. For example, a six-year Duke University study of four thousand men and women over sixty-four years of age and of various faiths, found that those who attended church regularly had a 46 percent lower relative risk of dying during a six-year period than those who did not attend. A Dartmouth Medical Center study of 232 heart-surgery patients found that one of the best predictors of survival was the degree of comfort and strength that they drew from their faith and through prayer. University of Miami research found that AIDS patients who were involved in religious practices and volunteer work were more likely to be long-term survivors.[1] The *Handbook of Religion and Health* concludes from this evidence that those who practice their religion, generally live longer, have lower blood pressure, show improved surgical outcomes, have shorter hospital stays, better mental health, and enjoy a greater sense of overall well-being.[2]

These outcomes could not be explained by other mediating factors such as health status, health behaviors, social support, and sociodemographic variables.[3] Dr. Redford Williams in *The Trusting Heart* reports that those who attended church regularly had lower blood pressure levels than those who attended less often. Williams quotes Dr. Berton Kaplan who observed, "Many aspects of religious observance could be health enhancing and disease preventing."[4] Williams goes on to note that Christianity as well as the world's other major religions "have as one of their core teachings the injunction to be less concerned with self and more concerned with loving others and treating them well."[5]

Praying Makes You Healthier

In *The Relaxation Response,* Dr. Herbert Benson references dozens of studies that demonstrate how prayer and meditation reduce stress.[6] Harold Koenig, a researcher and director of the Center for the Study of Religion, Spirituality, and Health at Duke University, has empirically demonstrated that men and women over the age of sixty-five who regularly pray and attend church have a "40 percent reduction in the likelihood of high blood pressure." He explains, "When people pray, their fear of death goes down. Equally important, active faith mitigates the grief over the death of a husband, wife, relative, or friend. The believer can cope better with a loss because he knows the loved one to be in God's good care." Koenig also found that elderly people who are not disabled are 47 percent more likely to die sooner if they are not actively engaged in prayer, meditation, or Bible study. Koenig goes on to describe how prayer and worship can help counteract the loneliness that often accompanies old age. He comments, "When you know that God is present you no longer feel that lonely."[7] Another recent study demonstrated that twelve- to fourteen-year-old boys who tended to "relinquish their problems to God and trusted that he would take care of any difficult situations" were less likely to use drugs when they turned ages fifteen to sixteen.[8] Koenig notes that prayer "boosts morale, lowers agitation, loneliness, and life dissatisfaction and enhances the ability to cope in men, women, the elderly, the young, the healthy, and the sick."[9] He continues, "While I personally believe that God heals people in supernatural ways, I don't think science can shape a study to prove it. But we now know enough, based on solid research, to say that prayer, much like exercise and diet, has a connection with better health."[10] Dr. Henry Newberg of the University of Pennsylvania has documented how prayer and meditation changes the blood flow in particular regions of the brain.[11] Walter Larimore, a Christian physician and author of *10 Essentials of Highly Healthy People* states, "If you choose not to be a spiritual person, then you are choosing to be less healthy than you can be."[12] And physician Larry Dossey says that "not using prayer on behalf of my patients was the equivalent of withholding a needed medication or surgical procedure."[13]

Perhaps the clearest explanation of the correlation between one's health and religion comes from Gary Gunderson, Director of Operations for the Interfaith Health Program of the Carter Center in Atlanta. He explains, "When we don't have faith—when the world doesn't make sense—our lack of coherence drives us toward destructive behavior in conscious and unconscious ways until that brokenness expresses itself in a way that can be described by the crude measure of health science."[14] When people experience wholeness through their relationship with God, they are at peace with the world, attuned to serving others, and focused on balancing their personal health. As a result, they are naturally healthier than those who do not understand their place in a chaotic world. Such lack of understanding often leads to self-destructive behavior, depression, isolation, and other unhealthy living patterns.

Our Relationship with God Matters

Duke University Medical Center and the Durham VA Medical Center conducted a study that examined 595 patients over fifty-five years of age. The results showed that those who felt abandoned by God, or who attributed their illness to the devil, had a higher mortality rate. Although it is too early to draw any definitive conclusions, Harold Koenig, a researcher on this study, comments:

This study is important because it identifies specific religious conflicts that may lead to poorer health and greater mortality, conflicts which may be readily addressed through pastoral interventions. Whenever anyone becomes suddenly ill with a disease that threatens life or way of life, they ask "Why?" "Why me?" It's not so much a question as it is a release of frustration. They experience anger at God for not protecting them or for not answering their prayers for healing; they feel like God is punishing them; they question God's love for them, and sometimes feel like others have deserted them as well. This is a normal and expected stage of grief over tremendous loss and life change. Most people, however, move through that stage. They soon are able to reconnect with God and with their spiritual community, and utilize these as sources for support and growth. Others, however, remain in that state and block themselves off from anything spiritual. These people are in trouble—and doctors need to know about it.[15]

It is of note that some medical schools in this country are now teaching students how to take a patient's spiritual history. Many in the medical community recognize that patients who struggle with their faith—or, in our terminology, are not living a life of wholeness—may be at a higher risk for unfavorable medical outcomes.[16]

The Type of Faith You Have Matters

Researchers have found that even the type of faith you have can determine to what degree your health is affected. They distinguish between *extrinsic* faith and *intrinsic* faith. Extrinsic faith is based on rules and externals. Those who possess an extrinsic faith value their faith because it meets personal needs. Extrinsic faith "tends to be reflected in the acceptance of social categories by sex, age, status, and external indicators."[17] Such individuals often selectively apply their religious codes in response to perceived societal threats. By contrast, God's Game Plan for Life assumes an intrinsic faith is at work—one that provides a framework for living and a basis for meaning in life. People who possess an intrinsic faith tend be less selfish, are more likely to follow the golden rule, and focus on societal needs. They also, as a rule, are more tolerant of different points of view and ideas. Those with an extrinsic faith are more likely to have a greater fear of death, experience more frequent illness, and are slower to heal. Those with an intrinsic faith recover more quickly from illness or injury and may, in fact, live longer.[18]

Being Connected to Others Makes Us Healthier

A vital aspect of God's plan is that we as individuals become a part of the greater whole. God created us to be in community, to interact with others, and thus to move toward wholeness for all. Intentional involvement with others has a direct positive impact on our health. *Health Psychology* reports several studies that support this conclusion. One reports that women and men who have extensive social contacts live an average of 2.8 years and 2.3 years longer, respectively. Another has found that single men who were heavy smokers died of lung cancer at a rate five times higher than married men who were also heavy smokers. And another study demonstrated that women with a strong support system are less susceptible to herpes, have fewer heart attacks, and have lower rates of psychological distress.[19]

Dean Ornish, physician and president and director of Preventive Medical Research Institute comments:

> The real epidemic in our culture is not just physical heart disease; it's what I call emotional and spiritual heart disease: the sense of loneliness, isolation, and alienation that is so prevalent in our culture because of the breakdown of the social networks that used to give us a sense of connection and community.
>
> So what? People who feel lonely and are isolated are more likely to smoke, to overeat, to abuse drugs, to work too hard.

Also, many studies have shown that people who feel lonely and isolated have three to five times the risk of premature death not only from heart disease but also from *all* causes when compared to those who have a sense of connection and community.[20]

Dr. Dennis Jaffe, in his book *Healing from Within*, says, "Evidence is mounting that over-involvement with oneself, at the expense of community, leads to psychological dislocation that results not only in anxiety but in various psychological ailments as well."[21] Jaffe goes on to say that for those whose lives are characterized by a joy, satisfaction, and trust in relationship with others experience a "positive physiological response that occurs throughout the body, particularly in the immune system."[22] The evidence is clear that connecting with and serving others as God intends makes us healthier.

A Concern for Others Makes You Healthier

Dr. John Porter is a New York–based psychotherapist who specializes in addiction. He explains that self-help and recovery groups, such as Alcoholics Anonymous, Overeaters Anonymous, and Narcotics Anonymous, are successful because of the natural healing that occurs when people demonstrate love and concern for others. He observes, "When a recovering addict comes to the aid of a confused, desperate newcomer, the helper's self-esteem increases and then is further reinforced by the gratitude of the individual being aided. In essence, people heal each other in a loving and supportive environment. They give of themselves unselfishly and they form a strong bond with the other members of their recovery group. The result of this activity is a restoration to a wholesome and sane life."[23]

The medical, spiritual, and mental health communities concur on the strong connection between the mind, body, and spirit. Medical researchers are now trying to determine what specific thought processes and actions have the most impact on our body's immune system. The early evidence suggests that a concern for others boosts our resistance to outside harmful influences. Let me cite just two of many studies. In the first, Harvard physicians David McClelland and Carol Hirshnet showed a variety of movies to subjects. The result was that those who watched a documentary on Mother Teresa's work with the dying showed an increase in immunoglobulin-A, our body's first line of defense against infections. Those that watched movies not pertaining to stories of compassion had no such change. In another study, McClelland found that people strongly motivated by a need for power often have lower levels of immunoglobulin-A than those whose motivation involves concern for others. He concludes, "This suggests that one way to avoid stress and illness associated with a strong power drive is to . . . turn the power drive into helping others."[24]

Volunteering and Giving Your Resources Makes You Healthier

Giving of ourselves to help others also includes giving of our material resources. The apostle Paul said, "It is more blessed to give than receive" (Acts 20:35), and, "God loves a cheerful giver" (2 Cor. 9:7). Douglas Lawson, in his book *More Give to Live: How Giving Can Change Your Life,* summarizes the research that demonstrates that giving of your resources and volunteering your time and energy in the service of others can make you healthier. He describes research on the brain's release of certain chemicals, called endorphins, when one is engaged in esteem-building activities such as volunteering and charitable giving.[25] Harvard cardiologist Herbert Benson explains that altruistic acts engage a relaxation response that is equivalent to a deep state of rest. *Psychology Today, American Health,* and the *Institute for Advancement* all confirm that we experience a "helper's high" when we serve other people.[26] The original research on "helper's high," conducted by sociologist Allen

Luks, studied fifteen hundred women volunteers. He found that many of the women experienced enjoyable physical sensations when they were volunteering, which reduced their emotional stress and improved their health. Luks found that by helping others many of these women stopped worrying about themselves, had a greater sense of calm, reduced anxiety levels, and a greater sense of self-worth.[27] A ten-year study of twenty-seven-hundred men showed that the mortality of those who regularly engaged in volunteer work were two-and-a-half times lower than those who didn't. Lawson concludes that, "Giving is not just a minor influence on good health but the key to physical and mental well-being."[28] Robert Schuller, whose church broadcasts the nationwide religious television show *Hour of Power*, concluded: "People come to life—become fully alive, aware, and joyful—when they help others. . . . God loves us when we love each other, when we share His love with other human beings."[29]

Having Less Stress in Your Life Makes You Healthier

The U.S. Department of Health reports that the three leading causes of death in America—heart disease, cancer, and stroke—are all stress-related. The medical evidence is clear: stress kills us sooner rather than later. The most interesting study, conducted Dr. Hans Selye, a leading authority on the effects of stress, suggests that the most effective philosophy of life in dealing with stress is the feeling of *gratitude*. Gratitude, more than any other emotion, helps us survive as humans and protects us in stressful situations. Selye explains:

> Gratitude is the awakening in another person of the wish that I should prosper, because of what I have done for him. It is perhaps the most characteristically human way of assuring security. It takes away the motive for a clash between selfish and selfless tendencies, because, by inspiring the feeling of

gratitude, I have induced another person to share with me my natural wish for my own well-being.[30]

Ludwig equates Selye's empirical findings on the benefits of gratitude to the biblical framework of wholeness. He notes:

> Selye comes close to a biblical perspective of the whole person, and, on the basis of scientific research regarding gratitude, seems to echo the proverbial wisdom: "If your enemy is hungry, give him food to eat; if he is thirsty, give him water to drink. In doing this you heap burning coals on his head, and the Lord will reward you (Prov. 25:21-22).[31]

Rachel Naomi Remen, physician, professor of medicine, therapist, and long-term survivor of chronic illness, relates a story about a woman with chronic heart disease and angina who experienced chest pain "when she was about to do or say something that lacked integrity, that really wasn't true to her values." Remen comments that this isn't surprising, noting that stress often attacks the weakest link in our physical and emotional makeup. In addition to raising the blood-sugar level in those who have diabetes, causing headaches to those who suffer from migraines, and stomach pain to those with ulcers, "stress may also be as much a question of a compromise of values as it is a matter of external time pressure and fear of failure."[32]

Intriguing information is coming out of the area of *psychoneuroimmunology* (PNI), a relatively new field that studies how our mind and nervous system impacts our immune system, how our body reacts to our imagination, fears, emotions, and beliefs. Ludwig elucidates, "It means that our religious faith is somehow connected with the cells of our body and the state of our physical well-being."[33] There is growing evidence that people who suffer from emotional stressors and who tend toward negative beliefs are at greater risk for developing diseases such as cancer due to the inability of a person's resulting weakened immune system to destroy the invading pathogenic germs. For example, researchers in the field have found that people who are naturally optimistic are healthier than pessimistic people. By comparison, those under stress—women who recently divorced, or those who have lost a spouse, students taking final exams—all had lower "killer cell" activity, leaving the body less able to fight off invading disease.[34]

Forgiving Others Makes You Healthier

Another aspect of living the biblical life of wholeness has to do with the ability to forgive. The following is a striking example. Amy Biehl was an intelligent, idealistic young college student who traveled to South Africa on a Fulbright Scholarship in order to assist in the anti-apartheid movement. She was tragically murdered by two men during a riot. Her grief-stricken parents decided to leave their upper-middle-class lifestyle in California to move to South Africa with the hope of carrying on the work of their daughter. The couple eventually met their daughter's killers, both of whom had been pardoned for the crime. The two men, full of remorse, by then were actively engaged in public service for a foundation Amy's parents had established in her name. Linda and Peter Biehl forgave their daughter's killers, and since have become friends with them, to the point that the two young men now address Linda as "Mom."[35]

Few of us could be so forgiving. We are all taught to forgive, but often we do not. Instead, we focus on revenge, or we associate forgiveness with weakness—and none of us wants to be seen as weak. Forgiveness has been defined as "the replacement of negative unforgiving emotions by positive other-oriented emotions (such as empathy, sympathy, compassion, agape love, or even romantic love).[36]

The empirical study of forgiveness is relatively new, but fast growing. By 1998, fifty-five separate studies had been conducted on the topic. While more work continues, social scientists have begun to quantify the power of forgiveness in several arenas. The bottom line is that not only is forgiving others the right thing to do, it also accrues health benefits to the one who forgives. In 1998, *ABC News* reported: "Studies show that letting go of anger and resentment can reduce the severity of heart disease and, in some cases, even prolong the lives of cancer patients."[37] The sorrow of the Biehls' loss will never go away. In forgiving the men responsible, however, the parents are now able to lead meaningful lives filled with hope instead of lives of anger and bitterness. By way of confirmation, Gregg Easterbrook, senior editor of the *New Republic,* points out, "Even when someone wrongs you, feeling anger or hatred only causes your life to descend into misery and resentment. You are the one who suffers, not the person you are angry at."[38]

Everett L. Worthington Jr., a nationally recognized psychologist and author of *Five Steps to Forgiveness: The Art and Science of Forgiving,* describes how a chronic refusal to forgive creates stress, and that those who are unwilling to forgive have more stress-related disorders, lower immune-system function, and worse rates of cardiovascular disease. Worthington also offers some thoughts about who is most likely to forgive, and who is not. Those who exhibit an empathic and agreeable persona are more likely to forgive then those who are characterized by anger, fear, worry, and who are emotionally reactive.[39] Worthington also found that people who forgive may be less clinically depressed, have longer marriages, and have healthier support systems. In turn, a longer marriage continues to improve overall well-being; partners who remain married longer are statistically healthier on most health barometers, including that of longevity.[40] Want to live a longer and healthier life? Forgive someone. It is yet another example of how following God's command improves the world and makes us healthier and happier.

Counting Our Blessings Makes Us Healthier

Recent groundbreaking studies at the University of California at Davis suggest that living in recognition of and appreciation for one's life and possessions improves physical, spiritual, and mental health. Psychologist Robert Emmons, coauthor of *Words of Gratitude for Mind, Body, and Soul,* reports on his twenty-year study on what makes people happy.[41] He found that, "When people consciously practice grateful living, their happiness will go up, and their ability to withstand negative events will improve as does their immunity to anger, envy, resentments, and depression."[42] Emmons also found that those who lived out of gratefulness tended to exercise more, were more likely to provide emotional support to others, and had better sleep patterns. The impetus for such gratitude, he suggests, comes from one's religious and spiritual life.[43] It is yet another compelling piece of research that supports our thesis that living a life of wholeness serves not only ourselves but all of humanity.

Adult Development Theory Sheds Light on God's Game Plan for Life

American psychologist Lawrence Kohlberg, in his theory on the stages of human development, proposes that humans progress through five developmental stages. Stage 1 is the stage of a very young child who views the world in terms of instant gratification and avoidance of harm. Stage 2 is achieved when a person becomes capable of assessing other people's needs and will occasionally satisfy their needs as a means of achieving their own goal—an "I'll scratch your back if you scratch mine" mentality. During stage 3, normally associated with adolescents, relationships with one's family, and especially one's peer group, become all-important. What is "good" and "right" is for the most part measured by the norms of the family of the peer group. Kohlberg labels stage 4, the "conscientious stage," at which a person begins to internalize the values of the larger society in which he or she lives. The emphasis in importance shifts from relationships to law, rules, and perceived obligations. Kohlberg personally believed that no more than 20 percent of the American population ever make it beyond this level. Other studies peg the figure at less than 10 percent. Those who reach stage 5 are able to examine critically their own values as well as those of society. At this stage, ŏne is allowed to move "beyond a duty-oriented mentality to become a truly autonomous moral entity."[44] One researcher explains the difference between stages 4 and 5 in this way: "The crucial new element is generativity, the commitment to generate a meaningful life for oneself through self-determination, self-actualization, and self-definition—the hallmarks of an autonomous person."[45]

James W. Fowler, in his book, *Stages of Faith,* proposes a sixth stage:

> Stage 6 is exceedingly rare . . . [People in stage 6 live] with felt participation in a power that unifies and transforms the world . . . The rare persons who may be described by this stage have a special grace that makes them seem more lucid, more simple, and yet more fully human than the rest of us.[46]

Before his untimely death in 1987, Kohlberg also began to theorize about the possibility of a sixth stage. He incorporated Fowler's definition, describing one who had attained this stage as having "a sense of unity with the cosmos, nature, or God."[47] Examples of people who fall into this category include Mahatma Gandhi, Mother Teresa, Dag Hammarskjöld, and Thomas Merton. While you and I may never be able to imitate Mother Teresa perfectly, God's Game Plan for Life provides us with the path that will bring our lives closer to being in unity with God. Each of us has the potential to know that "felt participation" with God through the integration of God's Game Plan for Life into our own lives. It is a power that will allow us to transform our own lives, the lives of others, and the world in which we live.

Similarly, others have described the correlation between one's developmental growth and their religious faith. E. F. Schumacher, in his book, *Good Work,* describes it this way:

> The human being's first task is to learn from society and "tradition" and to find his temporary happiness in receiving directions from the outside. His second task is to interiorize the knowledge he has gained, sift it out, keep the good and jettison the bad. This process may be called "individuation," becoming self-directed. The third task is one which he cannot tackle until he has accomplished the first two, and for which he needs the very best help he can possibly find. It is dying to oneself, to one's likes and dislikes, to all one's egocentric preoccupations. To the extent that a person succeeds in this, he ceases to be directed from the outside, and he also ceases to be self-directed. *He has gained freedom or, one might say, he is then God-directed.*[48]

Psychologist Allen Bergin's research demonstrates that people who are intrinsically religious rated higher in positive social and psychological traits such as self-control, tolerance, low anxiety, responsibility, a sense of well-being, sociability, intellectual efficiency, psychological-mindedness, and flexibility.[49] Bergin asserts that personality development and the development of religious orientation are "intertwined."[50] In the words of C. Michael Thompson, "It seems clear that adult development and spiritual growth support and further one another. *They may even be, at bottom, different ways of looking at the same*" (emphasis his).[51] Thus, there is well-documented data to support the validity of God's Game Plan for Life.

Longevity Studies Are Instructive

Over the years, scientists have studied communities that consistently outlive the rest of us. Some of the longest-lived people come from groups scattered across the globe, and of various ethnic backgrounds, including the Georgians in southern Russia, the

Vilcabamba Indians of the Ecuadorian Andes, the Hunza Valley community in Kashmir, and natives of Okinawa, Japan. Many in these groups not only lived past the age of one hundred, they experienced a high quality of life after reaching this milestone. Researchers found that these communities share similar habits and traditions, most of which mirror the principles of shalom. Dr. Walt Larimore summarizes these characteristics.

- They exercise regularly and consistently.
- They avoid highly processed foods.
- They eat a nutritious diet.
- They drink lots of water.
- They consume plenty of fresh fruits and vegetables.
- They avoid loneliness. (Relationships within their communities with neighbors, family, and friends are vital.)
- They practice and enjoy regular sex. (Usually in a mutually monogamous relationship, even after the age of one hundred.)
- They live with and depend on their extended families. (They are provided cradle-to-grave security and support.)
- They seldom use alcohol or tobacco products.
- They intensely respect their elders.
- They lead active, fruitful lives well into their second century. (There is no retirement. They may slow down a bit, but they never stop.)
- They emphasize relationships and harmony over the pursuit of wealth or success.[52] (A moderate, healthy lifestyle that emphasizes relationships, caring for one another and family over material gains and success).

Oriental Medicine Has Something to Say

Roger Jahnke, doctor of Oriental medicine and author of the book *The Healer Within,* explains that by incorporating traditional Chinese techniques, such as movement, massage, meditation, and breathing into our lives, we become healthier. He describes four methods for accelerating the healer within:

Awaken the medicine within, restore the natural self-healing capacity of the body, mind, and spirit. . . . Cultivate the influence of positive emotions, such as joy and accountability. Cultivate the influence of faith—faith in the "mystery," faith in science, and faith in what you have discovered yourself. Cultivate humor and fun. Neutralize anxiety, frustration, and fear. Seek the support of others, and serve others by supporting them. Listen for the stories and testimonials that confirm your inner potential to reach your preferred conditions and circumstances.[53]

Jahnke summarizes this approach via three simple strategies: self-respect, love for others, and the vision of a better world.[54] Eastern medicine is founded on the mind-body-spirit model. This ancient philosophy for living is, in may ways, in line with God's Game Plan for Life, and is but one lens through which we see God's divine intent for us more clearly.

Great Works of Fiction Contribute to Our Understanding

While living in Paris I checked out from the library at the U.S. Embassy a copy of Tolstoy's classic, *The Death of Ivan Ilyich*. In this story, Ivan, a government bureaucrat stuck in a loveless marriage, falls sick with an undiagnosed illness. He was a petty and bitter man; neither he nor his family lived a life of wholeness. As his illness progressed, his family began to resent more and more the annoying intrusion he had become. It was during this time—near the end of his life—that Ivan recognized how alone he was in this world and how isolated his life had become. The physical, emotional, and spiritual suffering he experienced forced him to confront the very nature of his existence. In the time before he died, Ivan came to a new understanding of his life's meaning, and died a contented soul. Dennis Jaffe speculates that Ivan's cancer may have been caused by the lack of wholeness in his life.[55] If Ivan had, in fact, discovered these truths earlier, he may have never been stricken with cancer and died prematurely. *The Death of Ivan Ilyich* is an example of how God can work through illness and other crises to bring us closer to God—of how adversity can indeed be a blessing.

Other works of art—Arthur Miller's play *The Death of a Salesman* and the movie *About Schmidt*—also come to mind as examples of the human struggle to find meaning in life. They relate with great insight the plight of those whose lives are shallow, insignificant, unhappy, and soulless. These works provide anecdotal confirmation of what the Bible has been telling us for centuries, and what modern scientific research confirms: the lifestyle choices we make—from diet and medication to faith and those with whom we relate—greatly influence our overall well-being. As Garth Ludwig describes, "When we deal with the emotional and spiritual pains of the sufferer, we are at the same time dealing with the maladies of the body. We cannot really separate the disease a person has from the illness that the person feels and the sickness experienced in the social system. The processes of healing run wide and deep."[56] In the language of this book, the processes of healing include incorporating God's Game Plan for Life into our own lives.

Next Steps

Among those who champion the mind-body-spirit connection is Harvard University's Arthur Kleinman, who believes that we are now beginning to understand that all human events are simultaneously mental, physical, and spiritual.[57] Likewise, Dr. Paul Tournier, a Christian physician, describes "positive health" and one's "quality of life" as a "physical, psychical, and spiritual unfolding . . ."[58] The evidence clearly validates God's Plan for Living well.

Now that we are armed with this knowledge, what comes next? What steps must we take to assimilate God's Plan for Living into our complex and overloaded lives? The following chapters will offer some specific ideas. We will discover how to make the most of biblical values to help find us balance as we care for our family, find significance in our work, and serve others in our community and in the world.

Journal Questions—The Evidence Supports the Game Plan

"We get sick when we forget how to be well."
—Anonymous

What does this mean in terms of how we are to live our life? Have there been times when you have become sick physically, mentally, or spiritually because you forgot how to be well? Provide an example.

"He who despises his neighbor sins, but blessed is he who is kind to the needy."
—Proverbs 14:21

Recall a time when you helped someone in need, and describe how it made you feel. What connection is there between your daily acts of service and your physical, mental, and spiritual health?

"To ward off disease or recover health, men as a rule find it easier to depend on healers than to attempt the more difficult task of living wisely."
—Rene Dubos

Why do we rely on doctors to cure us rather than on our own efforts to keep us healthy? Why is it so difficult for us to live wisely? What first steps can you take to live a life of wholeness?

"Illnesses hover constantly above us, their seeds blown by the wind, but they do not set in the terrain unless the terrain is ready to receive them."
—Claude Bernard

How does living a life of shalom keep us from getting sick? Describe the connection between your health and your faith. What steps can you take to strengthen this relationship?

"When a man dies, he does not just die of the disease he has . . . he dies of his whole life."
—Charles Peguy

What does this mean in light of shalom, and the recent medical research?

"Health is as contagious as sickness."
—G. Lloyd Rediger

Describe how this statement can work in our own lives and as we serve others.

chapter four

leading a life
of balance

What shall I do with my life? How much am I willing to give of myself, of my time, of my love?
—Eleanor Roosevelt

It is one thing to understand in theory what the Bible and the empirical evidence have to say about how to live a life of wholeness. It is quite another challenge to apply this framework to our everyday lives. As you scurry around in the morning, trying not to be late for work, yelling at your children for the third time to get out of bed, cleaning up yet another dog accident while talking on the cell phone to your Type A colleague who is wondering if you have seen the e-mail he sent at 6:00 AM, you probably will not take time to reflect on how you will spend the rest of the day living in shalom.

Those of us who head to work are bombarded with e-mails, phone calls, department meetings, and assignments with overlapping deadlines. Those who stay at home are overwhelmed by the neverending list of errands, sick children, household chores, and the constant requests to volunteer our time because "you have nothing else to do." At lunch you grab a burger at the drive-through on the way to your next appointment. After work you race to soccer practice and afterward order a pizza and help your kids with homework. By 10:00 PM you fall into bed, exhausted, trying to catch enough sleep so you can do it all over again tomorrow.

Take an Assessment of Your Life

The simple reality is that if we truly want to experience life at its fullest, we must be prepared to make changes in our daily game plan. We start by looking at how—or whether—our life right now is in balance. I define balance as purposefully leading the life that God intends for me. The five game plays are a strategy toward that end, guiding us toward physical, mental, and spiritual health:

1. Take care of yourself.
2. Care for the environment.
3. Serve others.
4. Let the Holy Spirit empower you.
5. Become friends with God.

Maintaining balance in our fractured, frenzied, stress-filled world is a precarious task at best. Even those who are acutely attuned to that idea get knocked off the balance beam. A couple of days ago, I was congratulating myself on my successful balancing act between family and work, when the combination of an ear infection, two urgent requests for help, and a minor work crisis landed me squarely on the mat. As a result, I was cranky, distracted, and exhausted—in a hole that I didn't crawl out of for several days. The "experts" tell us we would need eighty-hour days to meet all our goals for success in every arena of our life.[1] Because we cannot possibly do this, we tend to focus on one or two areas to the neglect of others: we become workaholics, at the expense of our family; we pay attention to our own needs, but can't find time to serve others; we spend the weekend unwinding at the lake, but don't take the opportunity for peaceful prayer and meditation.

I attended a conference of Christian CEOs at which we were asked to draw stick figures of ourselves, each limb in proportion to the amount of time we devoted to a specific area of our lives: the head represented our relationship with God; the left arm, time we spent with our family; the right arm, time we spent at work; the left leg, time exercising; and the right leg time we dedicated to replenishing our own emotional and creative reservoirs. To the surprise of few, most of us ended up with grossly disfigured caricatures of ourselves—a huge right arm attached to a shriveled body. The point was clear: we often shortchange our family and personal health for the sake of work. Others are consumed with the goal of being physically fit to the detriment of the rest of their personhood. They become self-centered instead of outward-focused.

The tendency to be self-absorbed doesn't stop when you reach age sixty-five. There are those who seem to have "checked out" upon retirement, spending their energy and resources on such things as golf, travel, and a second home, and relegating to the back seat a sense of responsibility for their neighbor or their world. Still others are driven to get ahead, accumulating power and wealth as a measure of their success.

Some individuals have been born into circumstances and conditions that make keeping their balance in life very difficult. I have a good friend who lives with depression. When her depression is untreated, she cannot even leave her apartment. But by taking her medication and exercising she is able to take charge of balancing her emotional wheel. Another friend was diagnosed early in her life with a form of Lou Gehrig's disease, which is slowly deteriorating her nervous system. Although the disease limits her physically, she has worked hard at developing the relational, spiritual, and emotional aspects of who she is. In this way she gives back in new and creative ways to her family and friends who care for her.

None of us this side of heaven is completely whole. We are human, and our human task is to continually be aware of our weaknesses, and work steadily to accentuate our strengths so that we can function as healthy people. We are more likely to be successful if we have a proven framework to assist us. We now turn to some examples from the Bible and strategies from the world that will help us balance our lives as we humbly serve and worship God.

What the Bible Tells Us

God never intended us to live focused solely on ourselves or solely on others. The Bible provides poignant examples of people whose lives are in balance, as well as those whose lives are out of balance. King David, after committing adultery and murder, remorsefully describes how his guilt has affected his physical, spiritual, and emotional health: "When I kept silent, my bones wasted away through my groaning all day long. For day and night your hand was heavy on me; my strength was sapped as in the heat of summer" (Ps. 32:3-4). By comparison, we find in Proverbs 31:10-31 an excellent role model of a woman who, by living a life of wholeness, has attained balance and lives a life of significance. Thomas Addington and Thomas Graves state:

> This woman got high marks from the customers in all the key sectors of her life. In the family area . . . her husband had full confidence in her (Prov. 31:11) and her children called her blessed (v. 28). Her business associates recognized that she was a wise investor (vv. 16 and 18), a conscientious employer (v. 15) and a hard worker (v. 17). In her community, she was known for caring for the poor (v. 20), and she was praised at the city gate for her "works" (v. 31).[2]

Despite her wide range of responsibilities, there is no indication that this woman's life is stressed or out of balance. In fact, verse 25 says, "She is clothed with strength and dignity; she can laugh at the days to come." She had developed a reputation as a woman who feared the Lord. She made room in her busy life for God, and the results were obvious.

The Bible instructs us to live joyfully, without anxiety (Phil. 4:4-7); to be good stewards of our time, money, and talents (Matt. 25:14-30; Eph. 5:15-16); to work with excellence (Col. 3:23); to attach ourselves to a community of believers (Heb. 10:25); and to raise our children in the training and instruction of the Lord (Eph. 6:4).[3] The question, then, is: What strategies can we implement to live the life God intends? What steps can we take to begin the process of incorporating God's Game Plan for Life into our daily lives?

Managing Our Energy

The first strategy is to learn how to manage our energy. Jim Loehr and Tony Schwartz, creators of the *Full Engagement* model and the *Corporate Athlete Training System,* have spent most of their professional careers working with the world's greatest athletes, as well as dozens of Fortune 500 executives, helping them manage their energy as the key to lasting high performance, health, happiness, and a balanced life. You and I can learn from this system that has taught tennis star Monica Seles, professional golfer Ernie Els, basketball great Grant Hill, and a host of others how to train in order to compete at the highest level. Adopting these techniques will allow us to take the first step necessary to be completely engaged in living a life of wholeness.

In Loehr and Schwartz's bestselling book, *The Power of Full Engagement,* the authors explain how overuse and underuse of our abilities can diminish the energy level in every area of our life. The key is pacing. They suggest that we think of our life more in terms of a series of short sprints, rather than a marathon, "fully engaging for periods of time, and then fully disengaging and seeking renewal before jumping back into the fray to face whatever challenges confront us."[4] In our language, leading a life of wholeness means developing a pattern of living that pays full attention to our personal rest, revitalization, and spiritual renewal as necessary for proactively serving others.

Loehr and Schwartz challenge us to strengthen our "muscles" in every area of our life. They state, "To meet increased demand in our lives, we must learn to systematically build and strengthen muscles wherever our capacity is insufficient. Any form of stress that prompts discomfort has the potential to expand our capacity—physically, mentally, emotionally, or spiritually—so long as it is followed by adequate recovery."[5] By systematically pushing ourselves for short periods of time in one area, that area becomes stronger and spills over into the rest of our lives.

The Importance of Rituals

The authors emphasize the importance of engaging in positive "rituals," or a pattern of behavior that gives structure and intentionality to our lives. For example, by following a healthy diet and exercising regularly you have already built a routine—or ritual—into your life. Likewise, developing close family relationships takes certain rituals, some of which we aren't even aware. And creating an effective organizational culture or giving priority to our relationship with God also requires rituals. Loehr and Schwartz offer a three-step process to help us think about rituals in our life. They ask us to:

1. Define our purpose: "How should I spend my energy in a way that is consistent with my deepest values?"

2. Face the truth: "How are you spending your energy now?"

3. Take action: Close the gap between who you are and who you want to be. Creating a personal-development plan that is grounded in rituals.[6]

The rituals we have created—consciously or unconsciously—either enhance or work against our goal to live a life of wholeness. Going to church, exercising regularly, volunteering our time, lending a hand to our neighbor, playing with our children and grandchildren—all are vital for living according to God's game plan. Conversely, we erode a life of wholeness by overworking, eating poorly, drinking too much, being consumed by oneself, neglecting Bible study, and watching too much television.

Following are some of the rituals I have incorporated into my own life in an effort to successfully execute the five plays of God's Game Plan for Life. These rituals may or may not work for you. My hope is that they will spark your imagination for you to create effective rituals for living out God's plan in your life.

Rituals That Enhance My Mental Capacity

We can deplete our mental capacity by not feeding it new experiences or new knowledge. I have adopted a lesson from my good friend, mentor, and colleague, Rev. John Nunes. John, a passionate and effective pastor in Dallas, an author and nationally recognized speaker, says that if you haven't learned anything new or met someone new every day, you haven't grown as a person. He has pushed me to expand my intellectual capacity by reading books I normally wouldn't, and to expand my circle of acquaintances as strategies to broaden my sphere of influence on issues about which I feel passionate.

This strategy has borne much fruit. I have read books on the Old Testament that gave background for this book. I have developed new relationships that have resulted in several board appointments, which, in turn, has enhanced my ability to serve those in need. I have also discovered the potential for growth through the possibility of failure. Applying to a new endeavor what I have learned from past mistakes keeps me mentally fresh.

Over the past twenty years, I have practiced law, taught and administered in academia, worked in politics, run a social service agency, and written two books. After almost ten years with Lutheran Social Services, including seven as CEO, someday I will be open to a new calling. With a budget of $70 million, one thousand employees, and programs in twenty-one cities, my talents are far from being underused. In fact, I am probably closer to overuse and the resulting burnout. The possibility of failure in a new endeavor (such as writing this book) can provide a certain energy that I wouldn't otherwise have. And I am finding that pushing myself to imagine new possibilities in my career has made me a better husband, father, and person.

Rituals That Enhance My Spiritual Capacity

Throughout my life I have underutilized my capacity for spiritual growth. By spiritual capacity I mean my becoming more attuned to my relationship with God and my ability to be as emotionally open and honest as I can be with myself and others. In the past I have rationalized my weakness in this area as my being a product of German descent: we seem to have an innate distrust of showing too much emotion. I come from stock that identifies with the man, who, as the old joke goes, loves his wife so much he could almost tell her.

Several years ago I began to realize that my sense of being spiritually disconnected was seriously impacting my whole being. Despite my years of religious upbringing, I felt distant from God. But the Holy Spirit worked to broaden my "spiritual scope" through books such as Billy Graham's *The Holy Spirit: Activating God's Power in Your Life.*[7] I also implemented several rituals in my life, which, in Loehr's and Schwartz's words, increased my spiritual energy. As an example, during my weekly overnight business trips I set aside time every night to read the Bible and pray. Fitting this in meant that I merely had to rearrange my time according to this new priority in my schedule. Watching only thirty minutes of *Sports Center* in the hotel room instead of my customary hour hasn't hurt me. God has used the extra time I spend reading and praying to strengthen my faith, which, in turn, has had a positive impact on every arena of my life.

Another ritual that I have recently added to my "training schedule" is listening to audiotapes of the Bible while I'm in my car. Again, it may mean missing a half-hour of talk radio in the morning, but I'm not sure that is necessarily detrimental. As part of their "ritual" to strengthen their relationship, John Nunes and his wife, Monique, take time to pray together every evening. John describes how this also provides each of them a window into the daily life of their spouse as they quietly listen to what is on each other's mind, including their concerns and thanksgivings in their prayers.

Rituals That Enhance My Physical Capacity

My first few years as CEO of LSS were challenging. We were going through a difficult period organizationally, and my job was overwhelming. My life included high-calorie meals with donors and other stakeholders, frequent travel, early mornings, and sleepless nights spent worrying about how to meet payroll and turn around a $2 million operating deficit. Those three years of overstressing my physical capacity took a toll on my body. Life for me back then wasn't a series of short sprints; it was a marathon. I had gained weight, and my cholesterol shot up to dangerous levels. My doctor made it clear that if I didn't change my rituals, I would suffer disastrous consequences. In retrospect, it was clear that I was not paying enough attention to my own physical, mental, and spiritual health.

I listened to my doctor's warning and have since incorporated two rituals that have worked wonders. First, I committed to making sure that at least two of the three meals I eat each day are healthy. Breakfast is easy. For lunch, I have to make a choice: if I have the enchilada and taco combination plate, then I must eat a healthy dinner. However, if I have a salad at lunch, I can relax and not be as careful about what I eat at night. I had a harder time with the second ritual, which was to exercise at least four times a week. This might be a jog before work, riding the exercise bike at lunch, or swimming at the end of the business day. Because this has become a routine part of my day, I find that when I don't work out, my body feels uncomfortable. It is telling me to stick to the ritual. It is even more important to exercise when I have a particularly hard day at work. Recently, I have been pushing myself to run three miles a day instead of my usual two. It wasn't that I was that tired after two miles—just bored. Adding the third mile has not only increased my lung capacity and strengthened my muscles, but it has benefited my spiritual and mental selves, as well. I feel better about how I look, have more energy throughout the day, and need less sleep at night. I have also seen a positive impact on my writing skills, as physical exercise increases blood flow to the brain, stimulating new thoughts and creativity. The extra ten minutes it takes to run is paying off in my overall capacity to function well.

Rituals That Enhance Our Family Relationships

I have already made clear how important I feel it is to pay attention to strengthening our relationships with those we love. My wife, Laurie, nine-year-old daughter, Sydney, and I have established a number of rituals to help keep our family strong. Weekly church attendance is one. Because I am out of town on the average of two nights each week, I make the most of the remaining nights I'm at home. We have agreed that no matter how busy I am at work, I will be home by 5:30 PM. I get up as early as needed in the morning to get my work done, and will occasionally finish up later in the evening or on weekends. However, 5:30 to 8:00 PM is sacrosanct. During these two-and-a-half hours, Laurie and I talk, usually over a glass of wine, and then later include Sydney in the conversation. We eat dinner together as a family, and make sure we leave time for two dogs, one cat, and a guinea pig. The television is never turned on, and we rarely answer the phones. And, once a week, Laurie and I go out on a date—without fail. This gives us private time to talk and keep our relationship fresh.

Sydney and I have also established some rituals. In the winter, we go to breakfast on Saturday morning while Laurie sleeps, then it's on to the park or a bookstore. In the summer, it's all about swimming, because that's virtually all you can do in the hot Austin sun. Year-round we engage in horseplay rituals—pillow fights, wrestling matches, and competitive board games. My goal is to continue to appreciate Sydney on her terms and be a part of her life. Through this purposeful interaction, I have managed to navigate successfully through the minefields of make-up, puppies, multiplication tables, imaginary boyfriends, and the latest fashions. I have discovered in my daughter an imagination that has opened my own eyes to new possibilities. And she, for her part, has decided that my life is pretty interesting for an old man, and has begun thinking about how she might serve others in her own life.

Paying attention to our family in these ways has meant that Laurie and I have had to give up other rituals that we held dear. We each limit the time we spend with friends. Laurie has temporarily placed her professional career on hold. We don't play golf or go fishing on the weekend, and we watch television only as a family. Making these small sacrifices is important for us during this formative time in Sydney's life. And our reward is a stable and loving family. Reward also comes in a greater satisfaction at work. In *Executive Values,* I relate how the research demonstrates that leaders who put their family first make better bosses, are more productive, well rounded, and creative.

Rituals That Help Operationalize God's Game Plan for Life

One ritual that stands out above all others in helping me integrate God's Game Plan for Life is my adoption of a new prayer life— one that focuses on others and not on me. I still ask for wisdom, strength, discernment, and healing. These are things I continue to pray for on behalf of others. But I find now that my prayer every morning is shaped by one question: "How can I serve you today?" This keeps my calling to serve God in focus. What started as a "forced" discipline has become natural, as I extend my prayers to include family, coworkers, friends, and neighbors. I ask, "Is there anything I can do for you today?" This daily ritual has opened my eyes to new opportunities to serve; following through on these opportunities has helped me to become more whole, and has made me a better father, husband, son, brother, coworker, executive, and friend. It has been worth its weight in gold, both figuratively and literally, as God has blessed our family and the lives of those we touch.

Doing and Being

The second strategy for developing an effective game plan for achieving balance is to pay attention to the "doing" and "being" aspects of our lives. The goal of this strategy is to strike a balance between what we do and who we are. Most of us—especially those in leadership positions—tend to do a lot of things; that's how a leader gets to where he or she is. But, in the process, one can too easily forget that successfully managing one's life in a balanced manner is, first and foremost, a matter of who we are. As a Lutheran Christian, I believe my identity comes as a result of my baptism into Christ. All that I am able to do flows from who God has made me. It is easy to confuse our "doing" with our "being." Take an assessment of your own life. How much of all that you accomplish is driven by your own expectation to perform—your need to succeed—and how much out of the sense of the assurance that you are loved by God, regardless of your performance?

I am not suggesting that our faith is an excuse for poor performance. Rather, it is our faith that enables us to exceed in all we do. We live more wholly when we build into our lives a rhythm of "being" that allows us to care for our own health and that of our family, and seek to do our best in our community and at our job. This means minimizing the nonessential stuff that clutters our life, and focusing instead on what is truly important.

Barry Johnson, an organizational development consultant, describes this dynamic of what we do and who we are as the "doing-being" tension. And it is exacerbated by our tendency to be self-centered. My waking thoughts are about me. How do I feel?

What can I do today to make my life a little easier? How can I sneak out of the office ten minutes early? How can I find a little extra time for myself today? Below is an adapted chart from Johnson showing the tension that exists between doing and being:

DOING	BEING
Positives	**Positives**
• Exploring new ways to serve others	• Rest, revitalization, and spiritual renewal
• Volunteering at your daughter's school	• Gaining perspective
• Counseling a family member or friend	• Acknowledging one's limitations
• Being strong for others	• Accepting oneself
• Witnessing to others through words and action	• Being grounded

DOING	BEING
Negatives	**Negatives**
• Burnout	• Spiritual narcissism
• Overextending oneself	• Becoming over-focused on one's self
• Neglecting one's own needs	• Isolation
• Neglecting friends and family	• Navel gazing
• Becoming cynical	• Loss of concern for others
• Being overwhelmed by problems	• Loss of sense of mission
• Becoming exhausted and humorless	• Hypochondria
• Physical or emotional illness	• Becoming part of the "me" generation
• Being at one's worst	• Excessive self-absorption[8]

Johnson calls us to face the truth. On what side of the ledger do our lives currently fall? Are we at risk of suffering burnout, or have we become so self-absorbed that we have stopped caring about those around us? Measuring our lives against the doing-being yardstick is helpful, regardless of our profession. I know pastors who work too hard to serve others at the expense of their family, health, and even their faith. I have also worked with pastors who fit the self-absorbed, narcissistic, "me generation" profile. I work with executives at publicly traded companies who give more back to their community and their colleagues than those who head nonprofit organizations. No matter what our position in life, we Christians must wrestle with how to achieve wholeness; how to find the proper balance, and create rituals that allow us to care for ourselves and for others; how to live out our faith fully without overextending ourselves to the point of exhaustion, disillusionment, cynicism, and burnout.

Life Is Meant to Be Enjoyed

When I become self-absorbed, it is usually because I'm trying to do too much. It isn't that I have stopped caring about the thousands of abused children our agency serves every day. I care, but one or more of the wheels of my self—physical, relational, or spiritual—has become unbalanced. My self-absorption often results in poor sleep, unhealthy eating, becoming sick. And my body is letting me know about it. It is telling me to take an evening or a day or a weekend or a week off in order to rest and renew, an opportunity to retool my mission and purpose. The point is to listen to your body, pay attention to your mental health, assess the health of your soul, and review your relationships at home and at work.

Sometimes, our hectic lives allow for just an evening of retooling. Occasionally, Laurie and I enjoy a three-hour meal and a bottle of wine at a favorite restaurant. Would we be able to do this on a weekly basis? Not if we want to honor our commitment to other vital areas in our life, like caring for our whole family, or tithing to our church. But we see these special evenings as a gift from God— pure joy in the celebration of good fellowship and good food. It is the message of the movie, *Babette's Feast,* in which a woman finds great pleasure in the careful and joyful preparation of an extravagant meal for her worrywart sisters. I see the occasional "extravagant" evenings Laurie and I share as a tangible reminder of God's gracious gifts of a loving and supportive family.

Our lives are marked by joy because our faith assures us of God's love. The full life we have floods down from God, filling us with joy that overflows in how we feel, how we look, and what we do. God has made us to celebrate life, to enjoy the fruits of the creation. We learn this lesson from the Bible, in which sumptuous feasts serve as a metaphor for the kingdom of God, the washing of feet with expensive perfume, the provision by Jesus of the very best wine for guests at the wedding at Cana—all reflect the abundant life we share as people of God.

Becoming Temporarily "Unbalanced" to Serve Others

There are times when we will need to sacrifice ourselves for the good of others—times when we choose to place our needs on hold (at the risk of temporarily losing our own balance) in order to serve our neighbor. Abigail Rian Evans describes this as "becoming broken so that others may become whole."[9] Bonhoeffer calls it "costly grace."[10] Roland Miller points to Jesus as our model: "Christ the Healer did not only suffer as he healed; he suffered in order to heal."[11] Our sacrifice might be staying up all night with a friend whose child has just died, helping a family whose home was flooded by torrential rains, volunteering for meals-on-wheels or Habitat for Humanity. Giving of ourselves in this way is vital to a life of wholeness that money cannot buy. It provides with opportunities to be the face of Jesus to the world. To paraphrase my colleague, Rev. Mel Swoyer, our actions are often the only Bible that some people will ever read.

All of these leave us winded, particularly when we are running our life in a series of sprints. We need time to renew—to gather our thoughts, commune with God—even as Jesus did when he went off by himself to pray. We rest. We engage in creative play with our family and friends. We worship God in church. We escape to the majesty of the mountains for a week of vacation in order to revitalize, gain perspective, learn, and be renewed. We become more aware of what comes between us and our mission—to "mind the gap," as the voice on the London Underground announces at each stop—between where we are and where we want to be. Taking time out in this way is not meant to be an act of selfishness that keeps us distant from others. Rather, in the words of Parker Palmer, "[T]rue contemplation is never a mere retreat. Instead, it draws us deeper into right action by getting us more deeply in touch with the gifts that we have to give, with our need to give them, with the people and problems that need us."[12]

Living a Life of Integrity As a Strategy to Achieve Balance

I have become sensitized to the signs that my balance is being threatened, whether physically, emotionally, spiritually, or socially. I know that I must pay attention to the "symptoms" of an unbalanced life. Am I getting enough sleep? Do I lose my temper too quickly? Am I as involved in community service as I could be? Are my family relationships suffering?

Since I have incorporated God's Game Plan for Life, I have become a better husband, father, employee, neighbor, and volunteer. And my overall health has improved. I still have a long way to go, and sometimes it seems like I take several steps back. But for the first time in my life I am at peace with my life and my God and secure in the knowledge that I am forgiven for my many missteps.

An added benefit of the lifestyle I have adopted is that I have a much clearer view of what is right and what is wrong in my life and in my decisions. God's Game Plan for Life provides healthy ethical boundaries that are easy to identify. That doesn't mean I never cross the line; however, I am much better at knowing when I do, and can take steps to keep me from digging the hole any deeper. I am also free to say "no" occasionally to those who want a piece of my limited time, even when their request is for a good cause. When my pastor asked me recently to help lead a capital campaign in our congregation, I declined (for the first time in my life!). I explained, "Our family will, of course, continue to support the ministry here, because we believe in it. However, saying 'yes' to your request right now would hurt my family and my calling at Lutheran Social Services." Having been there himself, my pastor understood that I was trying to be responsible for keeping my life in balance, and he graciously withdrew his request.

A reporter once asked the Indian leader Gandhi, "You have been working fifteen hours a day for fifty years. Don't you think you should take a vacation?" With his toothless grin, Gandhi replied, "I am always on vacation."[13] A strong sense of purpose kept Gandhi from burnout. A clear understanding of our purpose in life according to God's plan for us gives balance. It allows us to live a simple and joyful life of wholeness, as opposed to a complex, deceptive life of emptiness. It lifts up both our being and our doing in a manner that is healthy for our body, mind, and soul. A life of wholeness always begins and ends in Jesus, and his gracious invitation: "Come to me, all you that are weary and that are carrying heavy burdens, and I will give you rest. Take my yoke upon you, and learn from me; for I am gentle and humble in heart, and you will find rest for your souls. For my yoke is easy, and my burden is light" (Matt. 11:28-30).

Journal Questions—Leading a Life of Balance

"Life is the sum of all your choices."
　　—Albert Camus

　　How does Camus's quote relate to our attempts to balance our lives? What choices do we make that are harmful to achieving balance? What choices do we need to add in order to create a more balanced life?

"The search for happiness is one of the chief sources of unhappiness."
　　—Eric Hoffer

　　How can our unending search for happiness cause us to become unbalanced? How does it impact our physical, mental, and spiritual health? What, instead of happiness, should we be searching for?

"There is more to life than merely increasing its speed."
　　—Gandhi

　　How has the speed of your life impacted the quality of your life? What is important in life?

"That which does not kill us makes us stronger."
　　—Frederich Nietsche

　　Do you agree with Loehr and Schwartz that life is indeed a series of sprints? List some ways you can proactively strengthen your physical, mental, and spiritual selves by pushing yourself beyond what you normally do.

"We are what we repeatedly do."
　　—Aristotle

What aspect of your life do you most want to change? What training ritual can you implement to facilitate this change? Using Loehr's and Schwartz's three-step process, what rituals can you implement in your own life to improve your physical health? Your family relationships? Your relationship with God?

"The careful balance between silence and words, withdrawal and involvement, distance and closeness, solitude and community forms the basis of the Christian life and should therefore be the subject of our most personal attention."
—Henri J. M. Nouwen

On what side of the "doing-being" chart do you fall? What rituals will you implement in your own life to avoid becoming either self-absorbed or burned out from a lack of attention to one's self?

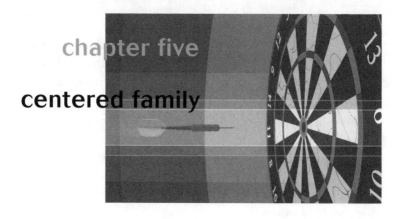

chapter five

centered family

If you bungle raising your children, I don't think whatever you do matters very much.
—Jacqueline Kennedy Onassis

You and I are called to serve God through our family, our community, and our work. The following chapters will explore these three ways of caring through the framework of wholeness.

Those of you who know me, or who have read *Executive Values,* know that I place a premium on the caring for family. I take seriously the admonition of Martin Luther, "Spiritual neglect of children is positively criminal. Nothing can more easily earn hell for a man than the improper training of his own children . . . if Christendom is to be helped, one must begin with the children. . . ."[1] These are strong words to ponder as we reflect on how we are caring for those we love most.

After ten years at Lutheran Social Services I have learned only too well how society has abandoned its children. I have witnessed firsthand the pain that abuse inflicts upon defenseless children. Parental neglect needlessly destroys lives and harms our society. Raising our children well must be our top priority. Mother Teresa, in a conversation with Rev. Arthur Simon, then executive director of the nonprofit organization Bread for the World, stated "In your country you have an even bigger problem [than hunger]. So many of your children are starved for love and affection."[2] Mother Teresa is right. Corporate America is demanding more of our time and energy in a culture that encourages us to be over-worked and overtired, with the promised reward of upward mobility and earthly possessions—all at the expense of our fami-lies. Laptops, BlackBerrys, and cell phones aggravate the problem with the seductive invitation to work at home and on vacation. The ideal employee these days has few family ties, but a great desire to achieve.

The result of it all is the devastation to our families, and to our children in particular. One large department store chain recently reported an 80 percent divorce rate among its manage-ment. Clergy and other church leaders are seeing their families disintegrate as members demand more and more of their time. Surveys show that teenage children of church workers report that they have no desire to follow their parent's career for fear of rais-ing their children in the same high-stress, highly visible homes in which they grew up.

The Cost—What the Research Says

We, as a society, have forgotten the importance of families. This lack of attention has had devastating consequences: over the past thirty years there has been a 300 percent increase in teenage sui-cide; a quarter of all adolescents contract a sexually transmitted disease before they graduate from high school; the divorce rate remains high; student SAT scores have declined; four million women are beaten annually by their partners; one in three chil-dren sleep in a home where his or her father does not live.[3] And 59 percent of our nation's children come home to an empty house after school.[4]

The simple fact is that mothers and fathers who are not physically or psychologically present in the home can cause their children devastating consequences. A recent study of early child-care conducted by the National Institute of Child Health and Human Development (NICHD) found that a correlation exists between the amount of time children before the age of four-and-a-half spend in daycare and the level of aggression, disobedience, and conflict with adults that occurs when these children reach kindergarten age and beyond.[5] Another study conducted by Columbia University's National Center on Addiction and Substance Abuse found that teens least likely to use drugs are ones that do the following:

- Eat dinner with their families at least six days a week
- Regularly attend worship services with their parents
- Attend a school where there is little or no access to drugs
- Are concerned about doing well in school
- Have friends who neither smoke, drink, or use drugs

The study found that teens are more likely to use drugs if their parents don't give them a specific curfew, assume their children will experiment with drugs, rarely eat dinner together, don't regularly attend worship services, don't think marijuana is dangerous, and blame their teen's drug use on society, media, or on their teen's friends. The evidence points to the inescapable fact that a parent's influence is the greatest predictor for drug use or lack of drug use among their children.[6] In homes where the father is physically or psychologically absent, children have a higher rate of asthma, anxiety or depression, and behavioral problems, are at greater risk for illegal drug use, and girls are three times more likely to engage in sexual relations by the time they are fifteen years old.[7] Another study reports that children who were less attached to their father by the age of five had lower self-confidence and were more anxious and withdrawn by the time they reached the age of nine. They were also less likely to be well adjusted in school and accepted by their peer group. Similarly, another study found that children of fathers who played with them in a "warm, sensitive, and challenging way" before they reached the age of two were more likely to form closer, more trusting relationships with others when they turn ten and sixteen.[8] *The Washington Times* reported that 85 percent of prisoners, 82 percent of teenage girls who become pregnant, 78 percent of high-school dropouts, and the majority of drug and alcohol abusers come from fatherless homes. No career or job should cause us to place our children at this type of risk.

One cause of these troubling statistics is a poor work-life balance. It is disheartening to realize the number of men and women who have sacrificed their families for the sake of their career. There are, of course, reasons why we work too hard. Sometimes we have no choice. Employees in a booming home-refinancing industry have felt compelled to work evenings and weekends in an attempt to keep up with the demand fueled by low interest rates. During the recent recession, many publicly traded companies laid off thousands of employees to enhance cash flow and earnings per share, leaving those remaining to pick up the slack. Some parents are forced to hold down two full-time, low-pay jobs just to make ends meet. Employees in the nonprofit world of human care are seeing their case loads expand—a result of the perfect storm of decreased government and private funding, reduced charitable giving, and more clients in need. In the postmodern world of work, there are no cookie-cutter solutions.

Single parents face even more daunting challenges. For most, work is an economic necessity. This doesn't mean that being a fully employed single parent will doom your children to be statistical failures. Burrowed within a difficult familial situation is a host of unique opportunities. As a role model, you are teaching your children the meaning of sacrifice and love. You live in an environment where it is natural to teach your children that they play an important role in contributing to the good of the family. Through example you can teach them how to be grateful and cheerful in the midst of challenges. It is also an opportunity to strengthen relationships with extended family as together you care for each other. Being a single parent requires sacrifice. Those who I know have time for their family, work, God, and little else.

As they are well aware, it is a demanding calling and chapter in their lives. However, as the research demonstrates, if your single-parent family is able to trust, love, believe in, help, comfort, forgive, work together, serve together, worship together, play together, and celebrate together, you are well on your way to providing a nurturing environment for your children.

But there are many who overwork because they choose to do so. A recent *Dilbert* cartoon depicts the pointy-haired manager at his desk on the phone with his wife, who informs him, "While you were working your children grew up and moved away." He hangs up, and silently congratulates himself, "I've never had a plan that worked so well." Arlie Russell Hochschild, author of *The Time Bind,* describes the "reversal model family" where "home is work and work is home." In her research on working women, Hochschild found that many preferred work over home. These women reported that they felt more appreciated at work, developed their strongest friendships at work, found mentoring their subordinates to be more satisfying than parenting their children at home, and, in times of crisis, found their coworkers more helpful than their family or church.[9] We are also drawn to work harder and longer by fatter paychecks, prestige of our position, and the rush that comes with closing a deal or making a sale. Philosopher Lee Hardy has written eloquently about what he labels the cost of work idolatry:

> In the wake of those in hot pursuit of professional advancement lie broken marriages, children filled with resentment, forgotten friends, and a God put on hold; those who race ahead often turn to alcohol to relieve the stress, or drugs to forestall burnout. Living in constant fear of failure, chained to the evaluations of others, their lives become filled with anxiety and caught up in a web of pretense. When an occupation is no longer freely taken as a way of responding to a call from God, it can be a cruel taskmaster indeed. Luring the unwary into portals of its temple with heady promises of worldly success, it

demands more and more of their lives and gives very little by way of lasting satisfaction in return. Those who initially devoted themselves to their careers as a means of self-fulfillment now find themselves entrapped and enslaved by a capricious and unforgiving god.[10]

Hardy observes that when a person crosses the line between working hard and becoming a workaholic, there is, in all likelihood, an underlying spiritual problem that isn't being addressed.[11] It is the sobering reality of the cost of forfeiting God's plan for our life. Of course, not every situation is the same; I don't pretend to be an expert in your particular circumstance. Sometimes the father has more flexibility to stay home, sometimes it's the mother. Often, it is a grandparent or an aunt. Each of us is responsible for making family our most important priority in whatever circumstance we find ourselves. We must ask ourselves, "How much job-related pressure can I withstand without compromising my family's physical, emotional, and spiritual well-being?"

Becoming Whole by Serving Our Family

The key to unlocking a life of wholeness lies in the health of our family. Allan Carlson, general secretary of the World Congress of Families II, observes:

> Our very identity as human beings impels us toward family life, toward marriage and children. A religious person would probably explain this as a consequence of Divine intent, in the Creation. The person of science could explain this as a consequence of 10,000 generations of human evolution. The conclusion, though, would be the same: to be human is to be familial.[12]

The research supports this conclusion. Married couples live longer, engage in less risk-taking behavior, have lower rates of suicide and alcoholism, become ill less often (and recover more quickly when they do), report less depression and fewer psychiatric disorders, are better off financially, and are more satisfied with their physical intimacy than those who are unmarried and sexually active. There is also evidence that children raised in strong, stable families are more likely to be successful, and to be physically, emotionally, and spiritually healthier.[13]

Living a life of wholeness demands that we care for our family. Derrick Bell, civil rights activist, attorney, and author, points to the fact that, even though we may be involved in "ethical" work, it is unethical to neglect our family and those we care about. Bell, Rev. Arthur Simon, Patrick Schiltz of Notre Dame law school, and many other successful people of high ethical standards have written publicly—and lamented privately—how their workaholic ways had negatively impacted those they love the most—especially their children. They realize now, all too late, that they will never be able to get back what they lost. Schiltz says bluntly that his behavior was wrong and unethical. Writing to fellow attorneys, he states:

> Being admitted to the bar does not absolve you of your responsibilities outside of work—to your family, to your friends, to your community, and, if you're a person of faith, to your God. To practice law ethically, you must meet those responsibilities, which means that you must live a balanced life. If you become a workaholic lawyer, you will be unhealthy, probably unhappy, and, I would argue, unethical.[14]

Note the language that Schiltz uses—a language of wholeness. His words are an admonition for us to live out our personal values in our family and in our work in order to be happy and healthy—in other words, to be whole.

Sadly, unethical behavior toward our families is evident also among leaders in the church, the government, for-profit and not-for-profit organizations. Far too often we hear how pastors and other church leaders have sacrificed their personal health and their family's well-being for the sake of their ministry. And they reap the harvest of such misplaced values—rebellious children, broken families, premature death, burnout, and sexual misconduct. Their divine calling, as important as it is, does not guarantee them a "get out of jail free" card for their offense. Studies conducted within my own denomination show that while, on average, Lutherans live longer and are healthier than the population at-large, Lutheran clergy are significantly less healthy. As congregation members, we have a duty to give our clergy the time and resources adequate to care for their family, as well as their own physical, mental, and spiritual health.

I attended the funeral of an executive who left behind a grieving widow and an eight-year-old son. It was clear to all of us who knew him that this tragedy didn't have to happen. His workaholic ways, job-related stress, and lack of physical exercise led him to an early grave. Sadly, he would have told you that nothing in his career was as important to him as his son. Had he known the tremendous burden his chosen pattern of living would have on his family, he would have done everything in his power to make the necessary changes. Unfortunately, he doesn't have a second chance. But we do. Regardless of our stage in life, how badly we have messed up, or our level of health, we are given a second chance. Our relationship with God through Christ guarantees forgiveness for the past, and strength to amend our ways in order to create a healthier family.

Not surprisingly, the research verifies that taking care of your family is good for your career, and that it is in an organization's best interest to care for the home life of its employees. A balanced family life and long-term organizational success are intertwined. A Dupont study found that employees who work for organizations that value a work-life balance were 45 percent more likely to "go the extra mile" for their employer.[15] Other studies have found that employees who live a balanced life—in addition to having a better family life—make better bosses, are more productive, more well rounded, more creative, and, overall, more effective. The lesson? If you want to become better at your job, work hard at having a balanced home life.[16]

The research clearly supports God's Game Plan for Life as a "framework of care" for your family. It has been shown empirically that families who are happy and successful tend to trust and love each other, help and comfort each other, forgive each other, work and serve together, worship together, and play and celebrate together. Moreover, families who are close to their extended families tend to be happier and more resilient when dealing with life's challenges.[17] Caring for family also measurably improves one's health. One study found that fathers who were involved in the lives of their children were more likely to be healthy. Another demonstrated that fathers who enjoy good relationships with their children incur less stress at work.[18]

Determining What Is Best for Your Family

Much has been written about the advantages or disadvantages of a mother who works outside the home as opposed to one who stays at home during her children's formative years. In reality, this is, at times, more a function of class than of choice; in many poor families, both parents must work in order to pay the bills. Of course, only you can decide what's best for your family. But the weight of the evidence in the studies I've seen seems to indicate that a second income may not be as beneficial as first imagined. In general, a person must make at least $30,000 through a second income in order to contribute one dollar to a family's spendable income. Although this may seem counterintuitive, the reasons are many. A second income can place a family in a higher tax bracket. Expenses may also increase, as more will likely be spent on such goods and services as childcare, work clothes, house cleaning, dry cleaning, eating more meals out, and "guilt" gifts from parents to compensate for spending less time with their children. Families are also often tempted to spend more on unnecessary items because of their higher income.[19] Often, the only noticeable difference resulting from both parents working is the increased stress level that comes with trying to do too much—which means that all members of the family suffer. Child psychologist James Dobson, asked to name the single biggest factor that has harmed families most, replied:

> It would be the almost universal condition of fatigue and time pressure, which leaves every member of the family exhausted and harried. Many of them have nothing left to invest in their marriages or in the nurturing of children . . . the two-career family during the child rearing years creates a level of stress that is tearing people apart. And it often deprives children of something that they will search for the rest of their lives.[20]

Many Americans are beginning to realize the benefits of leading a simpler life. From 1990 to 1996, 20 percent of all adults chose to have less income as one way to simplify their lifestyle. Eighty-five percent of those subsequently surveyed said they felt they had made the right decision.[21]

When Sydney was born, Laurie and I decided that it would be best for our family for Laurie to place her career on hold temporarily and be a stay-at-home mother. This has been a good decision. Laurie recognizes that staying at home is merely one of many chapters in her life, and that she can choose to pursue her career—when Sydney is older—without detracting from the health of our family. My mother chose to quit work when I was younger to pursue successfully a master's degree. Once I started school, she resumed her professional career; the right path for your family will depend on what you feel is most important for your household's health, and then make decisions accordingly. The decision process calls for honest reflection on your part about your reason for working. Is it to serve others and to provide care for your family? Or is it the result of social pressure or material desires? Perhaps it's a combination of both.

Advice from Experts (We All Are Experts)

Former U.S. Secretary of Labor Robert Reich, in his book, *The Future of Success,* tells about coming home from work early with the intention of asking whether his teenage sons wanted to do something. Sometimes, they would say "no thanks," their lives were full enough right then. Reich viewed this interaction from an economic perspective: he would forego earning money as a public speaker and author, expecting that the loss of extra income would be compensated in enhanced relationship dividends. I found Reich's perspective a disappointment in an otherwise insightful book. Our interactions with spouses and children cannot be reduced to merely a loss/dividend formula. I believe children easily sense if time spent with a parent is merely a matter of schedule, or if it comes from a mother or father being physically and emotionally available to them on a consistent basis, based on their rhythm and needs.

Creating strong family ties involves setting regular patterns of interaction, family traditions, and rituals centered around a strong Christian commitment. It is a way of living in the world. Reich has publicly admitted that the long hours he worked as Secretary of Labor took a toll on his relationship with his sons when they were younger—valuable time that cannot be recaptured. I have discovered that creating an ongoing relationship with Sydney means being present to her, constantly renegotiating my schedule and needs to meet hers in a way that will respect the time each of us has. That means I've had to learn to leave my CEO persona at work, where people jump when I ask them to do something. With children, it's different. I can't expect Sydney to drop what she is doing or thinking about in order to fit into my schedule; our time together in this developmental period of her life is worth the effort.

How do you know whether you are appropriately engaged in the lives of your children? It's the simple things: noticing whether they eat their pizza crust-first or not, tying their shoes, observing the mechanics of their baseball swing, knowing what they watch on television, or when they're surfing the Internet. Do you know who their friends are and what their parents are like? Can you describe their study habits, and be able to tell when they fib just a little about it? Do you know who their favorite musical group is or who they have a crush on? Quality parenting means knowing your kids as a baseball fanatic knows the statistics of every player on his favorite team. In *The Road Less Traveled,* M. Scott Peck argues that it is by these things children know they are valued. Being thus engaged in your children's lives also enables a parent to make minor adjustments based on such insight to guarantee that they receive love, discipline, education, values, and integrity.[22]

Here is the best advice I've heard about strengthening family relationships: If you want love, affection, attention, respect, and honesty from each member, you must offer the same. In other words, follow the golden rule, "So in everything, do to others, what you would have them do to you" (Matt. 7:12). If you want your children to listen to you, pay attention to what they have to say. If you want your spouse to be romantic and passionate, shower him or her with gifts, compliments, and the words, "I love you." If you want to forgive your parents for their weaknesses but can't seem to find a way, say the words to them, and chances are you will live into that promise.

I have had to be aware of reserving energy for my family. At the office is usually where we look our best, are on our best behavior, and have the most energy. It is also where others admire us for our skill and successes, giving us that extra shot of adrenaline. After ten hours of phone calls, several meetings, a couple of coffees at Starbucks with a working lunch sandwiched in, I often come home tired, exhausted by what took place at work. It is tempting to find a couch, the remote control, and a drink. It is tempting to check e-mails one more time. It is tempting to tell Sydney that I am too tired to play tonight. It takes real effort on my part to listen to what their day was like or to play a game with them—even when I don't feel like it. If I can find the energy for my colleagues at work, I can certainly find it for my own family. I pace myself on trips so that I don't come home weary. It is far better in the long run to say no to a colleague for a nightcap after a business dinner than it is to say no to a nine-year-old who wants to go swimming with her father. Roy Naturman, currently the head of the medical staff at Overlook Hospital in Summit, New Jersey, understands the importance of this commitment. During his residency, when he sometimes worked thirty-six-hour shifts, he would come home exhausted, but somehow still manage to read to his small son (at times, falling asleep as he read). In Naturman's words, his commitment "paid off. He's such an inquisitive kid."[23]

What Our Children Tell Us

As with other gifts from God, we squander opportunities to connect with our children, if we let an afternoon walk, laughing with them, playing card games, listening to their dreams and stories, and their daily experiences slip by. In bypassing these opportunities, we lose out on helping make their dreams become reality—dreams of a loving family, a life of significance, and a fully joyful life. What children want is not more toys, but time with us—with our whole selves. Even though they cannot put it into words, they crave for us to teach them how to incorporate God's Game Plan for Life into their own life so that they, too, can become whole.

Dayle Shockley, an author and instructor living in Houston, polled boys and girls between the ages of fourteen and twenty-one about their description of the ideal father. The following are the boys' responses:

• Spend time with me, just talking together.
• Don't be too proud to say, "I was wrong," and "I am sorry."
• Show affection to your wife by hugging her, kissing her and buying little things for her.

- Acknowledge my achievements.
- Punish me when I need it. When I don't get punished, I feel as if you don't care how I behave.
- Let me handle some difficult situations myself. It will help me become a man.
- Don't try to be macho or Mr. Wonderful. Just be yourself.
- I hate it when you show off in front of my friends. I don't want you to act like a teenager. I want you to act like a father.
- When I have a problem, sympathize with me.
- Take an interest in the things that are important to me. I may not want to play sports. That doesn't make me a sissy. I need you to love me for who I am not who you want me to be.
- Don't be ashamed to admit you don't know everything. It doesn't make you less of a man, but it does make you more believable as a father.
- Show me more kindness.
- Please don't provoke me by constantly nagging me about everything. It discourages me from trying to do better.
- Set a religious example for me and take me to worship regularly.

The following is what the girls had to say:
- Always love my mother.
- Love me unconditionally for who I am and respect the career I choose.
- Don't favor my brothers over me. And understand there are times when I need you to be just with me.
- Discipline me after your anger has subdued.
- Don't say one thing and do another. I hate hypocrisy.
- Work fewer hours, even if it means not having as many things. I prefer having your time over having things.
- Please don't yell at me. And don't yell at my mother.
- Share your interests with me. Take me fishing or hunting. Or teach me how to work on the car or how to operate a computer. Whatever you enjoy doing, include me in your world.

- Tell me you love me often but also show it by hugging me a lot.
- Please don't tease me when I am in a bad mood; respect my feelings.
- Make some good memories with our family by playing games, planning family vacations, or just laughing more.
- Don't be afraid to tell me no. It shows me you care.
- Tell me about how you learned some of life's tough lessons. And teach me how to do the same.
- Show your family more affection, both verbally and physically.
- Teach me about God and take me to worship.[24]

Children are smart, perceptive, and have a clear understanding of what they want their parents to be like. They are telling us to care for them wholly. This is both our responsibility and our privilege.

The Family Is the Last Line of Defense

We live in a society in which we are bombarded by media messages that sell us dreams that cannot be fulfilled. All we need to be happy and live forever is wealth, plastic surgery, jet skis, a Lexus, or an exotic vacation. Gary Gunderson adds ironically, "Buy this and you will turn back entropy, tame chaos, regain your lost choices."[25] As Stephanie Coontz describes in her book, *The Way We Never Were*:

> Only the family, it seems, stands between individuals and the total irresponsibility of the workplace, the market, the political arena and the mass media. But the family is less and less able to "just say no" to the pressures that emanate from all these sources, or even to cushion their impact on its members. . . . But very few people can sustain values at a personal level when they are continually contradicted at work, at the store, in the government, and on television.[26]

Children are at an even greater danger of being influenced by these misleading and harmful messages. Recall Lawrence Kohlberg's stages of human development discussed in chapter 3. Adolescents normally fall within stage 3, where "good" and "right" is measured mostly by the norms of the family or peer group. With the erosion of values in our children's peer groups as a result of media messages and other factors, our role as Christian parents is more important than ever. Laurie and I pay tuition to send our daughter to a Christian school fifteen miles from our home, even though an award-winning public school is within walking distance of our house. It is also one reason Rev. Daryl and Elaine Donovan of Sanibel, Florida, choose to homeschool their four children.[27] It is why countless grandparents have made a commitment to play an active and ongoing role in their grandchildren's lives.

If we, as family, congregation, and community, don't move to counteract this multifront assault on our children, we will lose them to an unhealthy individualism, drugs, sex, strained relationships, and a distant relationship with God. It is indeed a war. Laurie and I see our role as parents reflected in a scene from the movie *Saving Private Ryan*. In the movie, a group of soldiers risk their lives in order to ensure the safety of Private Ryan. When they finally find Private Ryan, they ask only one thing in return— that he live a life of meaning so that their sacrifice has added value to this world. We tell Sydney that we will sacrifice our time, our resources, our energy—even our lives—for her well-being. All we ask of her is that she care for others in everything she does. Sacrificing financial and personal gain for the sake of a life of wholeness with our children won't give us celebrity status. But, in so doing, we fulfill our God-given responsibilities as parents, and we add value to the rest of the world by raising servants of God. We will have followed the words of Joshua, "But as for me and my household, we will serve the Lord" (Josh. 24:15).

Journal Questions—Centered Family

"Your success as a family, our success as a society, depends not on what happens in the White House, but on what happens inside your house."
—Barbara Bush

What aspect of your family life do you want to change in order to better serve your family? What steps for taking action are necessary in order to achieve this goal? What negative factors in our society make it so vital for us to focus on caring for our family?

"Children have never been very good at listening to their elders, but they have never hesitated to imitate them."
—James Baldwin

In what areas of your life do you hope your children or grandchildren imitate you? What habits do you hope that they don't imitate? What rituals can you implement to insure that your good habits are passed on?

"Each of us will one day be judged by our standard of life—not our standard of living; by our measure of giving—not by our measure of wealth; by our simple goodness—not by our seeming greatness."
—William Arthur Ward

How does your life rate when measured by this yardstick? How does paying attention to each of these three categories impact the lives of each of our family members? In what category could you improve? What rituals can you implement to accomplish this goal?

"Help thy brother's boat across, and, lo, thine own has reached the shore."
—Hindu Proverb

How does caring for the members of your family benefit you?

"A hundred years from now it will not matter what my bank account was, the sort of house I lived in, or the kind of car I drove . . . but the world may be different because I was important in the life of a child."
—Simone Weil

Tell about a child in whose life you have made a difference. Which children could you become even more involved with?

"Imagine life as a game in which you are juggling five balls . . . work, family, health, friends, and spirit. Work is a rubber ball. If you drop it, it will bounce back. But the other four balls are made of glass. If you drop one of these, they will never be the same."
—Brian Dyson

Why is the family ball conceptually different than the work ball? Which ball are you in danger of dropping? What rituals can you incorporate in your life to insure that none of the four glass balls get dropped?

chapter six

centered community

If you don't go to somebody's funeral, they won't come to yours.
—Yogi Berra

A woman was at a stoplight in her minivan behind a yuppie businessman in a BMW, who was chatting on his cell phone, oblivious to the changing light. When the light turned green, she remained stuck behind the BMW and began cursing, ranting, and raving, calling him every name in the book. She blared her horn, and finally, just as the light turned yellow, realizing his error, the man waved once, and sped through the intersection. As the light turned red again, the woman realized she would have to wait for the next green light, which triggered another volley of expletives and horn honking. In the middle of her verbal assault, the woman heard a knock at her car window, turned and saw a policeman pointing a gun at her, asking her to get out of the car. The officer made her get into the squad car and took her down to the station. Stunned at what was happening to her, she was frightened and speechless. A few minutes later the police officer came back to her and apologized for the mix-up. He said, "When I saw you cursing, screaming, and honking the horn and observed the 'Choose Life' and 'Christian Schools Care' bumper stickers, and the fish magnet on the back of your car, I naturally assumed that it had been stolen."

All of us have been that woman; impulsive, unkind, damaging thoughts spring to our minds and out of our mouths. It might happen in traffic, at the grocery store checkout line, passing by a homeless woman and her baby, gossiping about a coworker, or saying something to our spouse we wish we hadn't. The good news is that God forgives our sins, and the Holy Spirit gives us the strength and will to make amends to others, and improve our community and our world. Taking advantage of these God-given opportunities is an integral aspect of our earthly calling, and is vital as we strive daily to execute the five game plays:

1. Take care of yourself.
2. Care for the environment.
3. Serve others.
4. Let the Holy Spirit empower you.
5. Become friends with God.

The Earthly Trap

So many of us are missing what God wants us to have in our lives. We are deluded into thinking that we are responsible for our earthly success. Billy Graham reminds us that this mindset is the reason Jesus said it was so difficult for the rich to get into heaven. Graham explains, "The burdens and cares of this world often interfere with our faithful walk before the Lord. In the midst of material prosperity we should beware lest we fall into the same pitfall as the Laodiceans, who incurred God's wrath and displeasure because they felt they had need of nothing because they were materially rich (Rev. 3:17)."[1] St. Paul picks up the theme in writing to Timothy, "Those who are rich fall into temptation and a trap and into many foolish and harmful desires that plunge men into ruin and destruction. For the love of money is a root of all kinds of evil. Some people, eager for money, have wandered from the faith and pierced themselves with many griefs" (1Tim. 6:9-10).

Arthur Simon, in his instructive book, *How Much Is Enough?* warns that money can corrupt and lead us away from God. Possessions, says Simon, may capture our heart, but cannot nourish our soul. Far too often they prevent us from achieving wholeness in our lives. The irony is that most of us don't think we are rich. In fact, we often feel as if we are barely getting by. *The New York Times* reports that "most of the 72 million American families feel they cannot make ends meet."[2] However, if you compare the average American income per capita of $30,000 to the 1.2 billion people in the world who live on less than one dollar a day, you have to conclude that we are indeed wealthy by earthly monetary standards.[3] Thus, the biblical warnings against materialism are just as applicable to you and me as they are to a billionaire.

Often we get so caught up in our professional, material, and personal pursuits that we forget the very real cost to us. Housed in the Lieden Museum in Zurich is a Hindu statue called a "Dancing Shiva." Shiva is the Hindu word for the masculine aspect of a Hindu god. The statue portrays Shiva dancing around a ring of bronze flames, and in his hands are the symbols of the spiritual life. One of Shiva's feet is high in the air, the other is supported by the back of a man on his knees, who is oblivious to Shiva, focused intently on a leaf in his hands. Like this man, we lose ourselves in our devotion to the material world and fail to realize the vibrant and living God dancing around us.[4] God's Game Plan for Life offers a structure to avoid this earthly trap. Our return to God when we have strayed comes by God's word of forgiveness, which leads to a life devoted to service.

Why Is It So Difficult to Get Involved?

One reason for our lack of meaningful involvement is our already stressed and complex lives, my own being an example. During the day I am a leader of a nonprofit organization. In my spare time I serve on the boards of three organizations, one a Fortune 500 organization, and two that provide care for the poor worldwide. I am also a husband, father, son, and brother. I help around the home, get involved at my daughter's school and with our church. In my spare time, I exercise, write books, travel around the country giving speeches, and pen op-ed pieces on issues of social concern. My wife has her hands full taking care of her daughter, husband, home, dogs, cat, and guinea pig, while also, on occasion, helping her sister, nieces, nephews, parents, and in-laws. She serves as room mother of our daughter's class, is active at church, volunteers at Lutheran Social Services, rescues stray and hurt neighborhood animals, and in her spare time is an actress, writer, painter, and does aerobics with her friends.

Our hectic lives are no different from yours. Although our many affiliations and responsibilities can release chaos into our lives, the rich and complex web of relationships we enjoy also provides us with enormous power and opportunity to broaden our scope of Christian service. Often, however, we use our involvement as an excuse not to do more. Sometimes we say no for the right reasons. But there are also times when we choose to shield our eyes, pretend someone in need doesn't exist, and haughtily rationalize away new commitments by pointing to our already overflowing plates.

Societal patterns also enable our unwillingness to become involved. In his well-researched book, *Bowling Alone: The Collapse and Revival of American Community*, Robert Putnam describes how our society is in danger of breaking down because we have become more disconnected from our families, neighbors, communities, and country. Putnam, a Harvard sociologist, uses the sport of bowling as an example. Years ago, it was common to bowl with others on a league. Today, we're more likely to bowl alone. Putnam explains:

> Television, two-career families, suburban sprawl, generational changes in values—these and other changes in American society have meant that fewer and fewer of us find that the League of Women Voters, or the United Way, or the Shriners, or the

monthly bridge club, or even a Sunday picnic with friends fits the way we have come to live. Our growing social-capital deficit threatens educational performance, safe neighborhoods, equitable tax collection, democratic responsiveness, everyday honesty, and even our health and happiness.[5]

Putnam's findings demonstrate the brilliance of God's Game Plan for Life by demonstrating that we are healthiest when our lives and the lives of those in our community are interwoven.

The Ripple Effect

Often we step back from community involvement, thinking that, as merely one person, we are insignificant and powerless to make a difference. You may have heard of the "butterfly effect" concept put forth by meteorologist Edward Lorenz. He asserts that the flapping of millions of butterflies' wings in Brazil can cause tornados in Texas.[6] This is a reminder of the power each of us possesses, how our individual and collective actions serve to make our world a better place, even though we may not be aware of the consequences of what we do. South African leader Nelson Mandela articulates the dynamic in this way:

> Our deepest fear is not that we are inadequate. Our deepest fear is that we are powerful beyond measure. It is our light, not our darkness, that most frightens us. We ask ourselves, who am I to be brilliant, gorgeous, talented, and fabulous? Actually, who are you not to be? You are a child of God! Your playing small doesn't serve the world. There's nothing enlightened about shrinking so that other people won't feel insecure around you. We were born to make manifest the glory of God that is within us. It's not just in some of us; it is in everyone. And as we let our own light shine, we unconsciously give other people permission to do the same. As we are liberated from our own fear, our presence automatically liberates others.[7]

Jean Rhys calls the dynamic between individual and community "feeding the lake," whereby each of us either adds to or takes away from this common source of human life.[8] We can apply Rhys's metaphor to our role as Christians. We, too, are charged with feeding the lake. Some, like Mother Teresa, Billy Graham, and Rick Warren are rivers and creeks that flow into its banks. Others are able to add only drops of water. Others, however, attempt to drain the lake by their self-absorption and neglect of others' needs. How much "water" we contribute isn't the issue; no trickle or drop is too small. What matters is that we make a conscious effort to feed the lake. Our calling is to serve, and there is no action—a kind word to a sales clerk, volunteering at the food pantry, accepting a church committee assignment, rescuing a frightened puppy, helping clean a polluted creek, going on a mission trip to Honduras—is too small. To feed the lake is to be a servant of Christ.

Getting to Know God through Serving Our Neighbor

Two of the game plays in God's Game Plan for Life are that we "get to know" God and that we serve others. Martin Luther says that, in many ways, these are one in the same: we encounter God through the needs of our neighbor. He cites Matthew 25:31-46, where Jesus identifies himself with the poor and needy. To turn away from them, says Luther, is to turn away from God, and to turn toward them in loving service is, in reality, serving God. When we, out of love, give money to the poor, take care of our elderly neighbor, or provide a mentally impaired child a chance to ride a horse, we are also giving our love to God. Theologian Paul Althaus writes, "For Luther, our love of God and our love of our neighbor cannot be separated."[9]

This is the behavior God expects. And, in so doing, our own body, mind, and spirit are strengthened. The Old Testament prophet Micah writes, "And what does the Lord require of you? To act justly and to love mercy and to walk humbly with your

God" (Micah 6:8). According to the New Testament, our acts of love are not only a pathway to our neighbor, but also to God. Christian writer Philip Yancey explains, "I do not get to know God, then do his will; I get to know him more deeply by doing his will."[10] Yancey quotes Thomas Merton who prayed:

> How shall we begin to know You if we do not begin ourselves to be something of what You are? We receive enlightenment only in proportion as we give ourselves more and more completely to God by humble submission and love. We do not first see, then act: we act, then see. And that is why the man who waits to see clearly, before he will believe, never starts on the journey.[11]

As stated in the introduction of this book, being a Christian is difficult. It means caring about the same things that God cares about—the poor, the environment, racism, injustice, the homeless, the persecuted. It means doing God's work within your community in order to know God more fully.[12] Such service can be an exciting journey; by it we become "little Christs," as Luther says. It is a living expression of the shalom—of the wholeness—that we enjoy with God and with our neighbor.

How Do We Begin This Journey?

Walter Brueggemann describes two consequences that come from living a life of wholeness:

1. We are expected to go where we are not.
2. We are expected to become who we are not.[13]

Living out of shalom changes our lives. Let me share with you a story about the journey of a friend who purposefully chose to go where he was not, and to become who he was not. This person isn't powerful because of his contacts, wealth, experience, or captivating personality. He is powerful because he simply wanted to make a difference. Rev. Matthew Harrison, a newly ordained pastor, was called to serve Zion Lutheran Church in one of the most troubled neighborhoods in Fort Wayne, Indiana. Although Matt possessed great intellect, he had no experience in working with the inner-city poor. He did not know how to deal with building-code violations, rat infestation, drug addicts, prostitutes, and vagrants. All he knew was that God had called him to serve in that environment.

Within a two-block radius of his church were some forty dilapidated, vacant homes and commercial buildings, most of which were occupied by the mentally ill, prostitutes, addicts, and others. Matt and the people of Zion partnered with their neighboring Roman Catholic church, St. Peter's, to make a difference. They refused to let a lack of money or experience discourage them. Together, they walked the streets to become familiar with every square foot of real estate and every player in this combat zone. They developed a plan to raise money from outside donors to purchase these properties and put them to better use. For three years they battled government bureaucrats, racist suburban whites, naysayers, inner-city land tycoons, apathy, vagrants, rats, stench, and a host of other opposing forces.

Their efforts bore fruit. All of the buildings were purchased, and many demolished to make way for construction of a public library, and of twenty-five new single-family homes. An apartment complex for seniors is on the drawing boards. Harrison reflects, "I have never felt more intensely the honor and privilege to serve Christ and his people than when I stood before his saints to give his gifts on Sunday, and then ventured out during the week as a representative of . . . Christ . . . to make a difference in one community, opening doors for the gospel, bringing light to darkness, and order to chaos, that the gospel might flourish."[14]

God led Matt where he previously had not gone, to become who he had not been. And God works to transform our lives through our first efforts at reaching out to others. Living a life of wholeness requires that we step boldly into places we have never been in order to serve others and to serve our Lord.

Begin with Your Family

Being involved in our community begins at home; we are to be available to each of our family members in their time of need. "If you want to save the empire, you must first save the family," Confucius said. We can be there to care for our elderly parents as they become less independent, for our nieces and nephews struggling through their parents' divorce, for our brother and his battle with alcohol, for our relative living in the darkness of depression, for the children of our cousin who is no longer able to parent due to illness.

Greg Singleton, chair of the Department of History at Northeastern Illinois University in Chicago, tells how what began as an empty, meaningless family gathering turned into a blessing for him and another family member. Greg publicly acknowledges the personal hell of his alcoholism and his sixteen years of recovery. A few years back he reluctantly traveled to Alabama for a family reunion. Once there, he was sorry he had gone. As Greg tells it, many in his extended family did not share his values, which meant there was polite, but boring, chitchat, instead of meaningful conversation. This way people could avoid discussing uncomfortable issues that might lead to arguments.

On the fourth day—when he was counting the hours until he could leave—Greg began talking to a daughter of one of his many cousins. He could sense the pain, anger, and sense of worthlessness that were all too familiar to him. Recognizing himself in her story, Greg asked, "Are you anesthetizing this with alcohol? I did for decades." As a result of their conversation, Greg delayed his plans to leave, and remained several days to counsel this woman in need. The two are still in regular contact, and she has been sober for more than five years. Greg says about that reunion in Alabama, "Lord knows, I tried to find excuses not to go, and frankly I came up with a few that were compelling. Why I went was a mystery to me at the time. It isn't now, and I shudder to think what would have happened if I had tried to figure the mystery out for myself, rather than let the Author show me."[15]

Continue by Serving Your Church and Community

One of our main tasks is to recapture the trust of our society by taking the ethical high road. And such trust is built on actions, not just words. We can proclaim the gospel of Christ until we are hoarse, but it won't make a difference if our collective acts of love don't accompany our words, together speaking volumes of what it means to live a life filled with Christ.

Our words and our acts are begun and supported by prayer. In asking, "Lord, how can I serve you today?" God opens our eyes to countless possibilities to bring healing to the abused, the forgotten, and the frail—like becoming a Stephen Minister, playing baseball with the boy down the street whose father has moved out, taking dinner to the neighbor whose daughter suffers from leukemia, inviting the neighbor children to vacation Bible school, praying with a friend who is trying to save her troubled marriage, speaking a kind word to our overworked pastor, and setting an example for our children by laying aside our needs to serve others.

Our congregations are an invaluable resource, a treasure of people and relationships from whom we can draw in our combined effort to "feed the lake." Gary Gunderson, in his book, *Deeply Woven Roots: Improving the Quality of Life in Your Community*, provides a road map for congregations to recognize and claim their unique role as a place of healing and renewal. A primary way congregations help is by connecting people with one another, and harness their collective power in service to others. This calls us to change how we view the purpose of our congregation. Many think the local church exists to serve us. It is there where our faith must get fed and our needs met. We expect a worship service to be entertaining, with a message delivered flawlessly and music that is pleasing to us, or we will take our business (our offerings) elsewhere. Those who follow God's Game Plan for Life turn the equation around, and ask: How can we best serve our congregation? What members need our assistance? Is there a way we can help our pastors accomplish their ministry so that they can maintain balance in their lives? What avenues are open to us for sharing the good news of God's love? Naturally, there are times when we need the support, services, and prayers of our brothers and sisters. But only by paying attention to the needs of others, as well as our own, can we live out God's Game Plan for Life, and thus be true to Jesus's command to love our neighbor as ourselves.

WDJD—What Did Jesus Do?

The task of community service through our "selves" and our congregation is a daunting one. A fair question is, "Where do I begin?" I have found that asking myself, "What Did Jesus Do?" (WDJD?) provides helpful framework for determining my actions. Note the difference in tense from the popular phrase, "What Would Jesus Do?" I credit Shannon Webster for using that twist of the phrase as an appropriate ethical guide. The difference, while subtle, is an acknowledgment that we needn't guess what course of action Jesus would take in a particular situation. Rather, we have in the Bible an accurate record of how he has already acted on behalf of others. He demonstrated his compassion for the poor, sick, lame, outcasts, and imprisoned. He showed genuine concern for his mother and modeled a healthy prayer life. His lessons of love in the Sermon on the Mount and his parables about lives of grace in the kingdom of God provide us with a wealth of exemplary experiences that we can apply to our own lives.[16]

The words and actions of Jesus—and the prophetic acts that pointed toward his reign—are the basis for Christian ethical decision making on complex twenty-first-century issues for which there is no direct biblical precedent—bioethical issues such as cloning and euthanasia, or our stance toward those of a different religion, culture, or lifestyle. The Bible "pushes" us past our comfort zone to go where we are not and to become who we are not, all for the purpose of engaging in a life of wholeness. For example, the story of the good Samaritan gives a clear ethical charge for us to dismantle the protective barriers we have erected to shield us from the pain and needs of others, and instead to serve our neighbor regardless of their skin color or religious belief.

I encourage you to consider prayerfully adding the WDJD ritual to your life. Make it a habit, when confronted with difficult choices, to ask, "What did Jesus do?" Sometimes he went off alone to pray, other times he entered into the joyful fray of good fellowship with friends and family. These examples reflect Jesus's "being" side. Out of this flowed his doing, as he served those who were in need of his compassionate gift of shalom. He simply asks that we be vessels through which his forgiveness and his mercy reaches others.

A Few Examples from All Walks of Life

No matter what our situation in life, each of us is in a position to serve. Age, material goods, marketable skills, a sour economy, family needs, injury, or illness—none of these is an excuse not to serve. Under God's Game Plan for Life, the only good time to serve is now.

Let me share with you a story about a colleague who turned a potentially negative situation to the advantage of others. During our time on the school board together, Scott told me that his work didn't satisfy the intellectual needs of a thirty-five-year-old Christian man who desired to serve others. At the time there weren't many other professional options available to him. Instead of becoming depressed about his situation or withdrawing from his responsibilities, Scott used the flexibility his job afforded him to work hard at his "job" of husband and dad, volunteering at his children's Christian school, his congregation, the local Christian college, and other nonprofit organizations. He continued as a solid worker in his profession, and remains a volunteer extraordinaire. Scott has made a far greater impact on his church and community than would have been possible if he were in a high-powered job. He cheerfully accepts his current situation in life, and uses his many talents to the fullest. Anyone who would look at his resume would not be overly impressed. But those of us who truly know the man know that what is on paper doesn't tell the whole picture. We whose lives he has touched by his example are grateful for his service. Scott understands that all the roles in his life are equally important. This is a lesson learned from the apostle Paul, who earned his living as a tentmaker but whose primary vocation was spreading the gospel of Jesus Christ.

We might also follow the example of Elaine Brundrett of Corpus Christi, Texas, who is "no one special," to use her words. Elaine floods her life with "simple" acts of charity. She teaches Sunday school and vacation Bible school in her congregation, is group host and choir member. She is a greeter, Bible study teacher, and shuttles elderly members of the church to the hospital. In her spare time Elaine coordinates an annual fashion show to raise money for abused children. She established and continues to volunteer at a "Points Store" at the Bokenkamp Children's Residential Treatment Center, where abused and neglected children earn points through good behavior. Children at the center can redeem these points for such hot-ticket items as Victoria's Secret hand lotion, Flaming Hot Cheetos, pickles, and *Seventeen* magazines. For many of the children, this is the first time they have had "money" to go shopping. Through these interactions trust develops and healing occurs. Elaine and the other volunteers witness by example, by word, and by deed.

If you visit the Bokenkamp Center, you may also run into Louis and El Doris Haverlah, a couple in their late seventies, affectionately known as Grandpa and Grandma. Instead of sitting at home watching television or reciting to others the burden of their aches and pains, Louis and El Doris spend a number of hours each week playing cards and board games with children, teaching girls how to sew, and just quietly listening as children share their struggles and fears. This couple's ministry is successful, not because what they do is extraordinary, but because they are intentional and authentic in being with the children. They understand that only after they establish a relationship of trust can any meaningful dialogue about personal faith in Christ occur. They view these children as their own, as fellow travelers in life. El Doris and Louis epitomize the words of Henri Nouwen, who tells us that the goal of ministry "is continually to recognize the Lord's voice, his face, and his touch in every person we meet."[17] They are living examples of how genuine service to others radiates from a life of wholeness.

Sharing the Pain of Others

The path to wholeness means that we must share the pain of others. It means empathizing with them in their physical, emotional, and spiritual injuries. Henri Nouwen describes this as being a "wounded healer." Nouwen illustrates why it is important to share each of this pain:

> When we honestly ask ourselves which persons in our lives mean the most to us, we often find that it is those who, instead of giving much advice, solutions, or cures, have chosen rather to share our pain and touch our wounds with a gentle and tender hand.[18]

Garth Ludwig adds, "The way of the Healer is to share the pain of others by entering into their world of shame and degradation. This is the theology of the cross!"[19] Bill Haley understands this commitment. Bill is involved with a mentoring group that serves children in Anacostia, one of the poorest and most dangerous sections in Washington, D.C. In explaining why he and his wife choose to live in the inner city to serve others, he responds, "Simply put: being a Christian means following Jesus. If our discipleship is not leading us to continue to give away our lives to other people, at great personal cost, then we are not following Jesus."[20] Being whole means getting to know your coworker, neighbor, and the person next to you in the pew so that you can be available to them in their time of need. It means staying up all night with a friend or family member who needs a companion in tough times. It means attending to the needs of the homeless man on the street corner, either by the active support of a homeless shelter or in a one-on-one relationship. It means sitting with the woman who has cancer whose family no longer comes to visit her in the nursing home. It means intentionally sacrificing yourself so that others may benefit.

But we can't do it alone. We enhance and extend our reach to others when we intentionally connect with overlapping webs of community that already exist. We can invite a friend to Bible study, include the new parents in your school's activities, make sure new members are asked to join your small group at church. Such interweaving of our overlapping connections strengthens every thread and creates a better, more whole community. As Gary Gunderson describes, "Every thread woven into the fabric strengthens it, makes its capacity more obvious and accessible to others."[21]

God has called each of us to be the salt of the earth and to let our light shine. Through our actions the world takes notice that we are, indeed, different, and that it is our Christian faith that makes the difference. Through our actions we live out the words of the song, "They will know we are Christians by our love." A life of service to others in our community is a reflection of God's Game Plan for Life.

Journal Questions—Centered Community

"One man gives freely, yet gains even more; another withholds unduly, but comes to poverty. A generous man will prosper; he who refreshes others will himself be refreshed."
—Proverbs 11:24-25

What new meaning does this proverb have for you as the result of your increased understanding of God's Game Plan for Life? How are you fulfilling this instruction in your own personal life?

"I am only one, but still I am one. I cannot do everything, but I can do something. I will not refuse to do something I can do."
—Helen Keller

Describe a time when a small act of kindness you did ended up having a big impact on someone else's life? Have there been situations where God provided you an opportunity to serve or witness and you didn't take advantage of this opportunity? What steps can you take to insure that future opportunities to serve don't pass by?

"In our era, the road to holiness necessarily passes through the world of action."
—Dag Hammarskjöld

How does this quote relate to our daily living when viewed through the lens of shalom?

"The world is not dangerous because of those who do harm but because of those who look at it without doing anything."
—Albert Einstein

Talk about the meaning of this quote in light of God's plan that we care for God's people and the world in the framework of wholeness. What specific actions can you take to become a better team player and fulfill God's desire that we care for God's kingdom?

"If anyone remembers me, it is because I was kind in confessional, I went to a wake, a funeral, or a hospital or wrote a letter at a particularly difficult time."
—Cardinal John O'Connor

Often it is the little things that count the most. What friend, neighbor, or coworker could use a kind word or action from you? Collectively, how do our everyday actions help spread the good news of God's love?

"Christ has no body now but yours
No hands, no feet on earth but yours
Yours are the eyes through which he looks
Compassion on this world
Yours are the feet with which he walks to do good
Yours are the hands with which he blesses all the world."
—John Michael Talbot

How does this song capture the essence of living out God's Game Plan for Life? How specifically will you use your feet and hands today to do good and bless the world? This week? This month? This year? List five people or organizations in which you plan to serve. Underneath each, list the action steps necessary to fulfill this desire. Next to the action steps write down the date that you will commit yourself to fulfill this commitment.

chapter seven

centered work

Focusing on ourselves will never reveal life's purpose.
—Rick Warren

When following God's Game
Plan for Life, we don't ask, "What do *I* want to do with my life?"
Rather, we discern what *God* wants us to do, how God intends us
to live. C. S. Lewis describes one's vocation as both a desire and a
duty. He states, "To follow the vocation does not mean happiness; but once it has been heard, there is no happiness for those
who do not follow."[1] Gilbert Meilaender adds, "We are not who
we think we are; we are who God calls us to be."[2] I have realized—belatedly—that the more I relinquish my own interests
and desires and focus instead on God's calling, the more I flourish and the more clearly I am able to receive God's next beckon-
ing. Flourishing may or may not be in the form of earthly
rewards, but it certainly means living a life of wholeness.
Listening for God's direction allows me to concentrate on what is
truly important as opposed to trivial things, thus giving significance to my life. Although choosing to act on that which is
important demands my daily attention, I find that it also gives me
a sense of peace—the conviction that I am in the right place at
the right time, doing what God wants me to do.

This hasn't always been the case. Going to law school was a decision born not out of prayer, but out of a desire for prestige, power, and money. As a result, the four-and-a-half years I practiced law were unfulfilling, to say the least. In retrospect, I understand that my mental and spiritual spheres were out of balance, vastly underused. Escaping to Paris for a year of study and reflection brought me closer to ascertaining God's will for me, but, again, I was still depending too much on myself and too little on God. Yet God was working through my educational and professional experiences to prepare me for the day I would discover my calling. Steeped in a background of politics and law, I was given the unexpected opportunity to be administrator of a small Christian university. There I learned from dedicated Christian role models and mentors about people management, budgets, and program development. I earned the least amount of money in my career there, but Laurie and I remember those years fondly because we knew that God wanted us there. I also began to understand the evolving nature of my call to serve religious organizations as a servant leader, board member, volunteer, and consultant.

I was thinking at the time that my next career move would be to step into the presidency of a larger Christian university. But, just then God again dropped another bombshell into my life in the person of Bob Greene, then current CEO of Lutheran Social Services. Bob stopped by to introduce himself one day and asked if I was interested in interviewing for his position, because he was anticipating his retirement in a few years. After much prayer, I began to feel God gently nudging me in that direction. I have been here now for ten years, during which time I have felt an intense deepening of my faith.

Out of this period of spiritual growth I felt called to write *Executive Values*. I had never written a book. I certainly didn't need to add another major task to my life. Despite my misgivings and the lack of a publisher, I embarked on the journey. Doors began opening. My board at LSS allowed me to take a sabbatical, and I found a publisher who was willing to take a chance on an unknown author. With its publication in 2003, I believe the book has, in some small way, furthered God's kingdom. Even as I write these words, I trust that God will use *Personal Values* to bless others, and am beginning to sense that it is time to keep my eyes and ears open to a new calling. I don't know where that will lead, but it is a challenge my family and I are eager to embrace.

What Is Work?

Our effectiveness in implementing God's Game Plan for Life depends, to a large degree, on how we understand our vocation. And that understanding hangs on how we define work. One of Martin Luther's most important contributions to the church is his insight of the two kingdoms of heaven and of earth. The kingdom of heaven is the kingdom of the gospel; through it God calls us to be in an intimate relationship through the merits of Jesus, and keeps this relationship alive by the working of the Holy Spirit in our lives. Christians belong to the kingdom of heaven, which we enjoy even here on earth. The kingdom of earth—the "temporal authority," as Luther calls it—is concerned with how we relate to others, how we use the earthly gifts God provides—schools, charitable agencies, community programs—to protect and enhance the life of others. We fulfill this duty when we behave responsibly as parent, child, spouse, volunteer, employee, neighbor, and church member. Our work, our calling, is located within the kingdom of earth.[3]

Through our various stations in life, God provides the opportunity and responsibility to care for our family; feed the hungry; clothe the naked; teach, heal, and protect the weak. Jacob Marley, in Charles Dickens's *A Christmas Carol*, exemplifies the spirit of caring for others through our work. Confronted by Marley's ghost, a terrified Ebenezer Scrooge says, "You were always a good man of business, Jacob," to which Jacob shouts back, "Mankind was my business! Charity, mercy, forbearance, and benevolence were all my business. The dealings of my trade were but a drop of water in the comprehensive ocean of my business."[4]

Robert Bellah defines vocation as that which "connects work's purpose with the proximate and ultimate end of a person's life," and bonds us to a larger community. The word *vocation* is from the Latin word that means "calling." It is God who extends our call to us.[5] For many of us, work is a place outside the home, where we go in order to fulfill our vocation—it is how we make a living. For others, work means staying at home, being mom or dad, and doesn't include a paycheck. These parents, by virtue of their being home, often have more time and opportunity to homeschool their children, care for their aging parents, and volunteer. Vocation, then, is something each of us has, whether or not we get paid for it. In fact, we have many callings. As a parent, one of my vocations is tending to my daughter's needs. As a spouse, my calling is to love my spouse and be an equal marriage partner. My other callings are CEO, author, board member, volunteer, and church member. In the living out of our vocations we express our wholeness.

God, through our various callings, continues the work of creation; we "participate" with God as cultivators and stewards of earth's resources. Each calling has equal value in God's eyes, whether cleaning our home, plowing the field, serving our congregation, managing a hotel, cleaning bed pans, or leading a Fortune 500 company. And each calling is sacred—through it we serve God and the common good. Luther says God even milks the cows through those called to perform those duties.[6] Paul Althaus, in his book, *The Ethics of Martin Luther,* elaborates:

> [S]ince the Christian has received the meaning and value of his
> life through God's gracious act of justification, all tasks and
> works of life are equally important and holy because they have
> been assigned to him by God's direction of his life. There are
> no particular holy works. Everything that we do is secular.

However, it all becomes holy when it is done in obedience to God's command and in the certainty that he will be pleased, that is, when it is done in faith.[7]

Within this framework, each of our vocations is on the same plane, for each has as its ultimate goal the service of others and the praise of God, even if our service demands personal sacrifice. Luther argues that every calling has its cross to bear, in that we discharge our duties for the sake of the common good, and in that spirit, suffer on behalf of others.

It Is Not the Type of Work That Makes a Calling

Over the years, hundreds of people have commented on how fortunate I am to be in a profession that serves those on the margins of society—children, the elderly, and the poor. Many have asked to work in my organization so that they might also make a difference. But, seen within the concept of work as delineated above, everyone can make a real difference in their current profession, working as agents of the mercy of Jesus to those around us. David Grizzle, senior vice president of corporate development for Continental Airlines, describes it best, "I find that if I am excellent in my professional work, it buys me wide berth to be fully who I am at work—in what I say, what I wear, and obviously, how open I am about my faith."[8]

In our post-modern twenty-first-century world many mistakenly equate money with value. We measure success by how much we make and not whether what we do adds value to someone's life. Sometimes we become so focused on getting ahead that we lose all sense of balance. The result is that a disproportionate number of people die prematurely each year from heart attacks, strokes, cancer, or other stress-related diseases, leaving behind a legacy of overwork, spending sprees, and broken families to show for their unbalanced, self-centered efforts. All of which results in *dis*-ease, or lack of health, as seen in the incidence of clinical depression and declining productivity. It is becoming clearer to us that psychiatrist Carl Jung was correct when he observed that meaninglessness is in fact equated with illness.[9]

One's vocation need not be a high-powered position to be God-pleasing. In fact, I believe it is often in the "menial" tasks that we serve God best. We sometimes forget that Jesus spent most of his adult life working as a carpenter. Consider the life of Betty Purdy, as reflected by Dinny, a character in John Galsworthy's novel, *One More River,* upon her death:

> Death! At its quietest and least harrowing, but yet—death! The old, the universal anodyne; the common lot! In this bed where she had lain nightly for over fifty years under the low sagged ceiling, a great little old lady had passed. Of what was called "birth," of position, wealth and power, she had none. No plumbing had come her way, no learning and no fashion. She had borne children, nursed, fed and washed them, sewn, cooked and swept, eaten little, traveled not at all in her years, suffered much pain, never known the ease of superfluity; but her back had been straight, her ways straight, her eyes quiet and her manners gentle. If she were not the "great lady," who was?[10]

Work Is More Than Just a Paycheck

The idea in our country that the sole purpose of work is to make money hasn't always been the case in American history. Our ancestors—many of whom were descended from Puritan or related backgrounds—brought with them the strong Calvinist notion of work as a calling. This Protestant work ethic is one reason our capitalist economy has outperformed that of most other countries. The harshness and excess nature of capitalism during this time was softened by the corollary Puritan doctrine that one's profits must be used for godly purposes. Although this concept persists in our collective social conscience, in practical terms, the idea of working to make money has been disconnected from any spiritual or religious significance. Sadly, the church over the past century has had little to say about this artificial split. What we hear from many pulpits on Sunday has little to do with any practical application for the rest of the week. Daniel Bell, in his book, *Work and Its Discontents,* seeing this trend, predicted that work will possess no intrinsic value other than to achieve a certain "standard of living."[11]

Fortunately, the idea of work as calling is making a comeback. Authors such as Robert Greenleaf, C. Michael Thompson, Laurie Beth Jones, Rick Warren, and Parker Palmer are raising our awareness of the biblical understanding. Ten years ago, only twenty-five organizations existed to help people reconnect their vocation with their faith. Today, more than nine hundred organizations worldwide have this as their focus. For example, the International Coalition of Workplace Ministries—made up seven hundred nonprofit organizations, for-profit businesses, and congregations—dedicates itself to learning more about God's role in the workplace.[12] Luther Seminary in St. Paul, Minnesota, has established a centered Life-Centered Work Initiative to equip Christians to live out their faith through their work. The H. E. Butt Foundation has created a Web site, www.thehighcalling.org, to help connect our faith with the "high calling of our daily work." *Business Reform* magazine and the Christian Management Association have similar goals. This rapidly developing broad-based movement has the potential to transform the workplace and create new opportunities for living a life of wholeness.

The Work Place Has Become Our Community

Collectively we have become more disconnected from the social fabric that has enmeshed and supported our communities. The result is that more and more people are turning to the workplace for a social support network. Boston University sociologists Dianne Burden and Bradley Googins, in a survey of fifteen-hundred workers, found that "the workplace is becoming the main community for people."[13] Chris Essex, a Rockville, Maryland, consultant on work-life issues, adds, "The work place has become the social support network we used to have in our backyards over the clothesline."[14] In an effort to meet this need, and as a strategy to improve employee retention, corporations today are creating new ways to connect employees in out-of-work settings, including golf leagues, investment clubs, prayer meetings, softball teams, and travel clubs. Some—Coca Cola, Intel, Sears, Ford, and American Airlines, to name a few—have established employee Bible study groups.[15]

The movement toward integrating faith and work provides new and exciting opportunities for Christian witness. Evangelist Franklin Graham comments, "God has begun an evangelism movement in the workplace that has the potential to transform our society as we know it." Kent Humphreys, CEO of a small business and of the Fellowship of Companies for Christ, an organization that ministers to Christian executive leaders, adds, "I have been at this workplace thing for about twenty to twenty-five years. I see a Kingdom mentality that has not existed until now. I see an openness of pastors and church staff that is very new. Church leaders are seeing God at work and want to know what is going on."[16] William Pollard, chairman of the multibillion-dollar organization, ServiceMaster, notes that in today's global economy the business community is the most effective means by which Christians can be "salt" and "light" to the world. *USA Today* adds, "In the twenty-first century, more religious leaders will be found in the corporation than in the conventional church."[17]

As an expression of our life of wholeness, you and I can further this movement through the purposeful integration of our faith into the workplace. In so doing, we demonstrate that being a person of God is the key to attaining significance in our earthly calling.

Money, Possessions, and Wholeness

Wealth does not equal happiness; it does not buy us meaning for life. However, some feel they need to choose among money, meaning, and success. Someone might be tempted to long for the life of the print tycoon Robert Maxwell. Maxwell's life of luxury allowed him to take a private elevator from his office suite in London to the building's roof. From there, he stepped into his helicopter, which took him to his private jet at a London airport, where he was whisked away to Gibraltar and a waiting limo that delivered him to his luxurious yacht, *Lady Ghislaine*, to leave port instantly and head out to sea. Overwhelmed by business problems, one day on board *Lady Ghislaine*, Maxwell committed suicide. This is obviously an extreme example, but it makes the point that wealth does not guarantee happiness.

Paul Johnson sheds light on that truth. When people acquire money, they are faced with two choices: they must either spend it "on competitive ostentation" or save it, and either choice brings with it its own set of problems and worries.[18]

One might ask: If wealth cannot buy happiness and wholeness, what's the point? Does our money serve us or are we slaves to our money? Is our higher pay the unintended consequence of our quest to serve God through our work or has it become the primary focus? Luther states that even a penny, when held close enough to a man's eye, can blot out heaven for him. He cautions, "When you have money, you will easily despise the God whom you also have."[19] God has much to say about our attitude toward money. The parable of how the servants handled their talents and the generous use of money by the good Samaritan for the sake of a stranger are excellent role models.

How we manage our possessions is serious business. When used as God intended, our resources are an invaluable tool for the care of others, and as one means by which we express God's Game Plan in our lives. Martin Luther describes it this way:

God does not want us to serve money and possessions. Nor does he want us to worry. But he does want us to work and leave the worry to Him. Let him who has the possessions be the master of these possessions. . . . [I]f he is master of the possessions, the possessions serve him and he does not serve them. When he sees a man who has no coat, he says to his money: Come out, young Mr. Gulden! There is a poor naked man who has no coat; you must serve him. Over there lies a sick man who has no refreshment. Come forth Sir Dollars! You must be on your way, go and help him. People who handle their possessions in this way are masters of their possessions. And, surely, all honest Christians will do this. But the folk who are saving much money and are forever scheming how to make the pile larger and not smaller are servants.[20]

Laurie and I see our resources as a gift from God that is meant to be shared. Our first priority is to tithe, giving back to God what is rightfully God's. Our second priority is to make sure that our family's needs are met. Third, we commit to using our resources to benefit others in ways that will not harm the environment. We strive to live our lives to serve God—not our possessions. Living by this set of promises frees us to simplify our lives so that we can focus on what is truly important. It enables us to accept jobs at lesser pay, and allows us to lead a balanced life of service. Most importantly, it brings us closer to God.

The African American leader W. E. B. DuBois, on the occasion of his ninetieth birthday, gave to his great-great grandson the following words of advice:

You will find it the fashion in America where eventually you will live and work to judge life's work by the amount of money it brings you. This is a grave mistake. The return from your work must be the satisfaction which that work brings you and the world's need of that work. With this, life is heaven, or as near heaven as you can get. Without this—with work that you despise, which bores you and which the world does not need—life is hell.

Income is not greenbacks. It is satisfaction, it is creation; it is beauty. It is the supreme sense of a world of men going forward, lurch and stagger though it may, but slowly, inevitably going forward, and you, you yourself with your hand on the wheels. Make this choice, then, my son. Never hesitate, never falter.[21]

These are truly words for us to live by, as well.

Finding Our Calling

Each of us is in a different place in terms of how we understand the relationship between what we do for a living and how we serve God—the dynamic between our profession and our vocation, or our calling. Some are searching for greater significance in their work. Others don't have the luxury of leaving their current job, but desperately want to add significance to their career. Still others are reasonably satisfied that they are carrying out their current calling in a God-pleasing way, but are looking for ways to serve where life next leads them. It is a misunderstanding—regardless of your current situation in life—to tell yourself that your "earthly" job will transform into a more meaningful vocation only when you discover your calling. As a worker called to live wholly, your first step is to assess your current position in order to find opportunities to serve others in creative ways: the customer who needs someone to listen, a coworker struggling through a divorce, a young single mom trying to escape poverty and care for her child by making it to the next corporate rung.

Your family also depends on you to discover and pursue your career as a calling. A sense of purpose in life makes one better adjusted, enhances marriage, and strengthens faith. It also increases work performance, and feeds your confidence to take risks in pursuing your next calling. Under God's perfect plan, work, faith, and family are interconnected to form a cycle of trust, meaning, and interdependence that moves constantly upward. In the words of C. Michael Thompson, "For those who view work as a calling there are no wrong turns, no derailments— just chances to grow."[22]

Po Bronson, author of *What Should I Do with My Life? The True Story of People Who Answered the Ultimate Question*,[23] listened to the stories of more than nine hundred people who took the leap of faith to follow their inner voice. His findings are illuminative. Bronson suggests that determining whether or not you have found your calling comes down to a simple gut check: "You either love what you do or you don't." He also found that one does not know what his or her calling automatically is. Most of the people he interviewed admitted they had made mistakes on their way to discovering what they were truly called to do. An investment banker became a catfish farmer. Before becoming a truck driver, one man spent years as a lawyer in the entertainment field. A police officer had first earned an MBA from Harvard. Bronson also found that, for most, settling upon one's calling came, not through major "epiphanies," but through whispers, a faint urge to follow their dreams. His study shows that waiting until you have achieved financial independence before pursuing your calling isn't a good strategy. Rather, he encourages people to embrace their dreams and develop the confidence to believe that you will be happy living within your means.

As Christians, we seek to embrace the dreams that God has in mind for our lives. What is it that God wants you to be passionate about for the next ten years? Once you find the answer to that, you have also likely found your calling. It enables you to talk about your vocation—whether what you are currently doing, or something in the future—in the language of significance. It allows you to see your daily work as part of the wholeness of your life—a gift far more rewarding than any monetary gain. Rich Karlgaard, publisher of *Forbes* magazine, elaborates, "We insult our Creator when we don't pursue what we were put on earth to do. We each come down life's gumball chute with a backpack of unique talents. Imagine, then, facing the Creator at death and hearing the words: 'I made you at this. You pursued that. What a squandering of potential.' That would be hell."[24]

Finding our calling depends on whether we are willing to set aside our own interests—in biblical terms, to approach God humbly and ask what God would like for us to do with our life. You may be called to the "mundane" job of working in a fast-food restaurant. It could be that you are asked to give up a life of material wealth to follow a less lucrative career. Perhaps you are being called to place your career as an accountant on hold so that you can take care of your family. Through prayer, the answer in your life will become clearer.

A life of significance comes our way when we use our talents as God intends. In the movie *About Schmidt,* the lead, played by Jack Nicholson, retires from a career as an assistant vice president in the actuarial department of a large insurance company. He is forced to come to terms with the fact that he never had the courage to quit his job in order to pursue his dreams. Instead, he chose the safety of a steady paycheck and a monotonous life in Omaha. We watch with sadness how he belatedly realizes how his lack of courage affected his relationship with his wife and daughter and sabotaged his emotional well-being. He retires, not knowing who he really is, or how he should fill his remaining days. The only thing that brings him a sense of purpose in life is a letter-writing relationship with a child who lives in another country, to whom he sends money through a charity he sees advertised on late-night television. Lessons about what it means to have a life of wholeness permeate this troublesome story.

I watched *About Schmidt* during a time in my life when I was pondering my own future vocations, ranging from the security of a steady income, to the scary thought of searching out my striking out in a new direction, which might mean less money. Out of my struggle came the realization that I could only walk the path of discovering my calling with the help of the Holy Spirit. The

Spirit is the "comforter" and "enabler" that Jesus promised, who would allow me to set aside my own thoughts of what I should be doing with my life and seek God's will. To take this leap of faith is like working without a net—you are in free-fall. But the alternative is ending up like Nicholson's character, living a life devoid of meaning.

I have met plenty of people who have taken this leap—and far too many who have not and will likely end up like Schmidt. I am not aware of a single person who, after doing so, wished they hadn't. If you are married, and your spouse is considering taking the leap, I suggest that you encourage it with much prayer, making sure there is a game plan. Then urge your spouse to follow the "whispering" of God. Any monetary sacrifices you may have to make will be made up through a sense of newfound purpose in your life as you grow toward wholeness. By finding his or her true vocation, your spouse will begin living out his or her calling, which will translate into stronger relationships at home and better health for all.

Sometimes We Catch a Glimpse of God through Our Work

Our work is a manifestation of our faith as we strive to serve others, but it is also a window through which we can see God. When I stress over the right words for a chapter in a book, or with the right decision to make dealing with an employee matter, it is through prayer that I trust the Holy Spirit is leading me. Catherine Marshall tells the story of how, while trying to hang drapes, she couldn't get the design to match the proportions of the windows. Frustrated, she left the scene and mulled over her dilemma in prayer. Before long, she had her solution, and through that experience, she says she learned that "Jesus is maestro of interior decorating."[25] Dallas Willard says our failure to have faith that Jesus can help us do our work often causes "our efforts to fall far short of what they should accomplish, and may even have less effect than the efforts of the Godless, because we undertake them only with 'the arm of the flesh.'"[26]

Rev. Ben Patterson, dean of the chapel at Hope College in Holland, Michigan, tells of the revelation he had while sitting through a worship service during the day when he served a parish. It had been a very tough year, and the thought struck him that he no longer enjoyed serving as a pastor. The choir was singing a beautiful anthem, and Patterson describes how, for a brief instant, he caught a glimpse of "God's transcendent beauty and goodness." His first thought was, "Lord, you are enough. I'll do this lousy job forever if you let me walk with you and get just a peek at you once in a while."[27] He put into words the reason any of us work: our daily toil provides us with a path to God. It is often a tortuous road full of detours and potholes, but staying true to the journey makes the end result worth our effort. Patterson explains, "There is no pain or perplexity so heavy that they outweigh his glory. And it would seem that both are necessary for us to see it."[28]

We Must Take Back the Workplace

Implementing God's Game Plan for Life means living a life of integrity in all that we do, including our work. The word *integrity* comes from the Latin word for "whole," or "entire."[29] It means that we act in a way that is consonant with our beliefs and values. There are times when we must summon up the courage to say, "No, I won't do that. It is simply wrong. I won't fudge accounting data. I won't backdate invoices. I won't shortchange a customer. I won't cut corners. I won't backstab my colleague. I won't attempt to discredit my opponent."

The collapse of the Houston-based energy giant Enron resulted in the destruction of $70 billion in wealth. Congressional hearings and court proceedings detailed a complex web of deceit and illegal activity designed to defraud thousands of investors. During visits by Wall Street analysts, Enron employees would make imaginary phone calls and negotiate imaginary trades. These misdeeds were not limited to company executives, but extended throughout the organization. David Skeel Jr. comments, "Some of the excesses of Enron can be addressed by regulation. But the rest comes down to business ethics and individual morality—the commitment of ordinary men and women to resist the often subtle temptation to sin."[30]

Acting with integrity is not only being true to ourselves and to God; through our collective efforts we are being true to the needs of others. By working together, fifty million Christians who currently serve in the American workforce have the power to reimagine our capitalist society. Writing in *Fast Company*, Robert Simons, Henry Mintzberg, and Kunal Basu comment that society simply won't work if we only care about *what's in it for me*. They state that we need to be people of courage for whom integrity and self-respect are absolute and are not open to negotiation. Here's what they have to say about what our society needs:

> [People] who won't sacrifice long-term interests for short-term gains, financiers who walk away from unethical deals, consultants who level with their clients no matter what, athletes who won't endorse useless products, and professors who refuse to bend the truth as expert witnesses.[31]

Such actions also give a positive witness. Others notice ethical people. Individuals who refuse to compromise their integrity attract a crowd of silent admirers. Through our words and our deeds, Jesus is revealed to those around us. How we act *does* matter. Sheldon Vanauken says it best:

> The best argument for Christianity is Christians—their joy, their serenity, and their completeness. But the strongest argument against Christianity is also Christians. When they are somber, joyless, when they are self-righteous and smug and

complacent consecration, when they are narrow and repressive, then Christianity dies a thousand deaths.[32]

If we answer our call from God by adhering to our Christian values and doing our best job, the world will clamor for our talents. By acting with integrity, each of us "reintroduces" Christ into the workplace. Collectively, we have the power to extend the message of the gospel to thousands.

Living a Life of Integrity Can Be Costly

Sometimes your colleagues will respect you for your honest morals: you will enjoy a higher status for doing the right thing. The same holds true for organizations. Research has proven that organizations are more likely to succeed over the long term when they adhere to their stated values. From a community perspective, our collective actions, motivated by our common desire to be genuine to others, benefit all of society. From a health perspective, studies have found that acting with integrity makes us well-balanced persons in body, mind, and spirit.

There are times, however, when if we are true to ourselves, people will mistrust us and criticize us. You may become the subject of whispers at the water cooler, and it may even cost you your job. At such times, we may think that our circumstances spell the end of the world as we know it. Such a perspective certainly *feels* real. But our Creator is well aware of our circumstances, and promises to bless us. As the apostle James declares, "Blessed is the man who perseveres under trial, because when he has stood the test, he will receive the crown of life that God has promised to those who love him" (James 1:12).

Taking such a long-term view of our lives gives us the patience and hope necessary to weather hard times. A Chinese proverb asks, "Can you remain still, while the water is turbid and cloudy, until in time it is perfectly clear again?"[33] The apostle James adds, "Consider it pure joy, my brothers, whenever you face trials of many kinds, because you know that the testing of your faith develops perseverance. Perseverance must finish its work so that you may be mature and complete, not lacking anything" (James 1:2-4). By choosing to ignore our values, we compromise our wholeness at the high cost of physical, mental, and spiritual health.

From a biblical perspective, acting with integrity is the only course. Jesus, who lived every moment of his life with complete honesty, makes it possible for us to do the same. His death and resurrection guarantees forgiveness for our failures, strengthens us to follow in his footsteps, and keeps hope alive. He says, "For whoever wants to save his life will lose it, but whoever wants to lose his life for me and for the gospel will save it. What good is it for a man to gain the whole world, yet forfeit his soul?" (Mark 8:35-36). Following the way of the cross means complete personal devotion to him. In *The Cost of Discipleship*, Dietrich Bonhoeffer says, "When Christ calls a man, he bids him come and die."[34] We figuratively die with Christ, die to our sinful ways, so that we might learn to live in his likeness here on this earth, and in eternity. Before he met his death in 1945, at the hands of a Gestapo execution squad, Bonhoeffer lamented that one can no longer tell the difference between a Christian and "an ordinary human life." He explains:

> To endure the cross is not a tragedy; it is the suffering which is the fruit of an exclusive allegiance to Jesus Christ. When it comes, it is not an accident, but a necessity. . . . Jesus says that every Christian has his own cross waiting for him, a cross destined and appointed by God. Each must endure his allotted share of suffering and rejection. But each has a different share: some God deems worthy of the highest form of suffering, and gives them the grace of martyrdom, while others he does not allow to be tempted above what they are able to bear.[35]

Being a Christian means living a life of integrity no matter what the cost. Losing our life for Jesus's sake means that we empty ourselves, even as he did so in order to take on human flesh. But in that emptying we find our true life. Wayne Muller describes how true freedom comes when we become "nobody special":

> We do our work not for glory and honor, but simply because we must, because we believe in the value of right action and good labor. In the end we may or may not receive our reward from the world. More often, we receive our reward in secret. During a quiet walk, when we suddenly feel lighter; when we receive a kind word, and the heart is made warm and full; during a moment's reflection, when we feel a clarity of purpose, in these and a thousand other unexpected ways, we secretly receive our reward."[36]

And, consider the story of Mulla Nasrudin:

> Mulla Nasrudin was eating a poor man's diet of chickpeas and bread. His neighbor, who also claimed to be a wise man, was living in a grand house and dining upon sumptuous meals provided by the emperor himself.
>
> His neighbor told Nasrudin, "If only you would learn to flatter the emperor and be subservient as I do, you would not have to live on chickpeas and bread."
>
> Nasrudin replied, "And if only you would learn to live on chickpeas and bread, as I do, you would not have to flatter and live subservient to the emperor."[37]

The Earthly Costs of Succumbing to This World

We overlook the potential consequences of false living only to our detriment. Just ask Betty Vinson. Betty was an accountant by profession and a Sunday school teacher in her congregation. She was happily married, with one daughter, and living in Jackson, Mississippi. In 1996, she took a job as a midlevel accountant with WorldCom. When her supervisors began asking her to input false accounting entries, Betty, at first, balked, but subsequently caved in. Besides the pressure from her superiors, she was afraid of losing her good salary and benefits; she and her family were living the middle-class dream. But her dream soon became a hellish nightmare. Today, the Vinson family is virtually broke due to legal bills. Betty, having plead guilty to charges of conspiracy and securities fraud, is awaiting sentencing.[38]

Contrast the road Betty took to the decisions made by Guenther and his wife, Rosemarie. I recall Guenther from my days as a child attending Grace Lutheran School in River Forest, Illinois, where he was janitor. Guenther was a huge man, who, in my young eyes, could do it all, and did do it all. He mopped up the mess after a first-grader got sick in the hall, cleaned the cafeteria, where Rosemarie often served as the cook, mowed the grounds, shoveled the snow, cleaned the bathrooms and fixed the broken desks. What I remember most clearly about Guenther was his pure joy in life: he seemed happy no matter what he was asked to do.

Wanting to know more about this man I admired so much, I asked my parents one evening about Guenther's background. Guenther and Rosemarie had escaped from East Germany during the Second World War, leaving behind their families, a successful career, and their possessions. Now, they were working as a janitor and a cook at a school an ocean away from home. The sacrifice was worth it, the couple said. What they gained in return was priceless: a newfound self-respect, a deepened faith, a clearer understanding of their values, and the freedom to worship openly and serve God seven days a week by caring for the children and teachers at Grace. From their perspective, this was the highest calling they could have.

Were they overqualified for their positions? Absolutely. Did they let this stop them from serving God to the best of their ability? Absolutely not. Had they discovered, through prayer and perseverance, their calling, and with it, a sense of peace and a life of wholeness? Without a doubt.

What Is Your "Rosa Parks Decision"?

Parker Palmer ties our life of integrity to our need to make what he calls our "Rosa Parks Decision," that is, a conscious choice to no longer act in a way that contradicts a deeply held truth. The story of Rosa Parks has become a symbol for the power of one person to transform society. Her one act that sparked the firestorm of the civil rights movement came on December 1, 1955, when she sat in a bus seat that was reserved for whites. When asked later to explain her action, Parks responded, "I sat down because I was tired." Reflecting on the incident, Palmer observes that her soul, heart, and her whole being was tired "of denying her soul's claim to selfhood." According to Palmer, she made a clear choice: "I will no longer act on the outside in a way that contradicts the truth that I hold deeply on the inside. I will no longer act as if I were less than the whole person I know myself inwardly to be."[39] What is your Rosa Parks decision? What truth do you feel compelled to cling to against every attack?

Derrick Bell, in his autobiography, *Ethical Ambition,* says his choice to live according to his ethics—to live with integrity—opened the door to professional success and a life of wholeness. Not every decision he made along the way was easy. He voluntarily stepped down from a faculty position at Harvard, where he was the first African American law professor to receive tenure there. His decision came as the result of the school's refusal to hire a female of color to join the faculty. Reflecting on that tumultuous time in his life and its meaning for his life today, Bell says:

> Miraculously, when I stand up and speak out, expressing an unpopular view strongly, fully aware that it is neither welcomed nor likely heeded by those in authority, I experience a unique sense of peace. It is that peace that I wish for my students and children more than anything else. I know more powerfully than ever that inner peace is worth more than

succumbing to apathy, and more than material gain. To risk ethically is a difficult blessing, but whatever the outcome, to risk ethically is also to live.[40]

Obedience Provides Freedom, Opportunity, and Insight

Ethicist Gilbert Meilaender observes: "The story of Jesus's own obedience makes clear that what looks like an annihilation of the self, may, in fact, be its enlargement."[41] The closer we are able to approximate Jesus's obedience, the closer we come to understanding that our actions, far from being merely a rote response to God's command, are a response to God's love. We respond to the question, "What does God want me to do with my life?" in the freedom of God's grace, knowing that, even when we fail in our attempts at obedience in our service to others, we are forgiven. At the end of the day, that assurance is the only thing that matters; it is what gives our life ultimate purpose. In seeking God's kingdom first, we place ourselves in God's hands, trusting that God will provide for all our needs. Whatever measure of earthly blessings we enjoy comes from living a life of purpose. As a writer once said, "You know what you want, so that is how it will turn out for you."[42] When we live, speak, and act with integrity, we give public expression to our faith, and, along the way, will have mined even more deeply the treasure of our peace with God.

Journal Questions—Centered Work

"For whoever wants to save his life will lose it, but whoever loses his life for me and for the gospel will save it. What good is it for a man to gain the whole world, yet forfeit his soul?"
—Mark 8:35-36

What implications does this passage have for you in terms of how you approach your daily vocation?

"I find that doing the work of God leaves me no time for disputing His plans."
   —George MacDonald

How does one know whether she is doing the will of God through her vocation? What process will you go through to assess whether you are currently doing the will of God?

"I long to accomplish a great and noble task, but it is my chief duty to accomplish small tasks as if they were great and noble."
   —Helen Keller

What daily tasks in your vocation provide you with the opportunity to serve others? How can you better take advantage of these everyday opportunities to serve even more and to serve them better?

"The real test of a man is not when he plays the role that he wants for himself, but when he plays the role destiny has for him."
   —Vaclav Havel

Why has God chosen you to be in your particular job at this particular time in your life? What future role does God have in store for you? How can you differentiate between discerning the role that God has in mind for you versus the role that you would like to fulfill?

"Preach the gospel always; and when necessary use words."
   —Saint Francis of Assisi

What opportunities are there through your vocation to spread the gospel of Jesus Christ?

"I am not a bad man; I'm just a bad wizard."
    —The Wizard of Oz

Why is it impossible, under God's Game Plan for Life, to compartmentalize our life? How can being a good Christian also make you a good employee? What ramifications does leading a life of wholeness have on how we perform our work?

conclusion

Everyone who hears these words of mine and does not act on them will be like a foolish man who built his house on sand. The rain fell, and the floods came, and the winds blew and beat against that house, and it fell—and great was its fall!
—Matthew 7:26-27

In an interview on the TV series *The Actor's Studio*, actor Nicolas Cage related how rock star Jim Morrison once lamented that he had never fulfilled his dream of writing a song that conveyed pure happiness.[1] Cage shared his dream of someday playing a role that "conveys pure happiness." From the perspective I've taken in this book, a screenwriter could portray such a character only if she understood God's gift of wholeness. God's Game Plan for Life allows us to come as close as humanly possible to experiencing pure happiness this side of heaven. God willing, it will be you or me whom Cage plays when he finds such a role.

Our striving toward wholeness is not unlike the story of Jacob. Recall how, being alone after sending his family to continue their journey, he wrestled with a man throughout the night. After a long, bitter struggle, light is beginning to appear on the horizon, and, realizing he is losing, the man touches Jacob's hip, crippling him. Still refusing to let him go, Jacob demands a blessing from the man. "Your name will no longer be Jacob, but Israel," says the man, "because you have struggled with God and with men and have overcome."[2] It is then that Jacob realizes he had been striving against God.

Perhaps you feel as I do—as though I have been wrestling with God most of my life. There are times we think we have the upper hand, but then God touches us through the stress, illness, heartbreaks, pain, and trauma. Broken and humbled, we realize that God's purpose comes out of mercy; we learn that the struggle ultimately brings blessing. We are "successful" in our striving toward wholeness because we have faith that Jesus, in his own struggling, has overcome our own. Jacob called the place where he wrestled "Peniel," or "face of God." In the same way, God becomes present to us most clearly as we follow Jesus—bearing our cross—in a life of faithful adherence to God's Game Plan for Life.

We must proceed without all of the evidence, without having proof that God is acting for our good. In the words of Dennis Covington: "Mystery is not the absence of meaning, but the presence of more meaning than we can comprehend." What gives me hope as I strive to lead a life of wholeness is God's promise always to lead me closer to God—in hard times and good. I don't understand why a ninety-eight-year-old man with dementia must writhe in pain from the cancer that has overtaken his body, but I catch a glimpse of God as nursing-home staff bathes, feeds, and loves this sufferer. I don't understand how parents can sexually abuse their seven-year-old son, but I see God at work as we provide help, healing, and hope to his shattered life. I don't understand why my friends John and JoAnn were struck with a chronic, painful disease at such an early age, but I experience first-hand God's mercy and awesome power when I witnessed my three-month-old daughter miraculously brought back to life from the clutches of death.

The Temporal and Eternal Consequences

Make no mistake, as we stand at the fork in the road—the one that demands no sacrifice or the path of the cross—our decision is not to be taken lightly. There are tremendous temporal and eternal consequences in choosing either. A Hasidic story tells about a man who prayed, "O God, let me know Your true name, even as angels do." God felt compassion for the man and granted his request, whereupon the man hid under his bed and cried in sheer terror, "O God, let me forget your true name." God granted this prayer also.[3] Similarly, God allowed Moses only a glimpse of God's true nature, saying "[You] cannot see my face, for no one may see me and live" (Exod. 33:20). Like Moses, we become more familiar with God as we fulfill God's desire for us to seek balance in our lives, serve others, and act as good stewards of the earth. And, from this path of following Jesus in a life of wholeness there is no turning back.

"[A]ll come from dust, and to dust all return," says the Preacher (Eccles. 3:20). Between those two end zones is what we call life. During these sixty minutes of game time we are called to choose right or wrong, good or evil, selflessness or self-centeredness, God or Satan. In God's Game Plan, God calls us to make the right choices. For those who do, life will be a revolution. J. Heinrich Arnold offers this insight: "Discipleship . . . demands everything—the whole heart, the whole mind, and the whole of life, including one's time, energy, and property—for the cause of love."[4] Jesus warns against choosing not to follow him, "Not everyone who says to me, 'Lord, Lord,' will enter the kingdom of heaven, but only he who does the will of my Father who is in heaven" (Matt. 7:21). God promises wholeness to those who do God's will, "I have set before you life and death, blessings and curses. Choose life so that you and your descendants may live, loving the Lord your God" (Deut. 30:19-20).

Despite these clear instructions, we often fail. Parker Palmer, in *Let Your Life Speak*, says it is sometimes easier to choose "death in life, exempting ourselves from the challenge of using our gifts, of living our lives in authentic relationship with others."[5] This choice not only exacts a toll from us, but it also harms others. Palmer explains this unintended outcome as the result of not linking selfhood and service. "If we are unfaithful to true self, we will extract a price from others. We will make promises we cannot keep, build houses from flimsy stuff, conjure dreams that devolve into nightmares, and other people will suffer . . ."[6]

The Paradox of Receiving Life by Giving It Away

Choosing wholeness results in a life filled with paradox. In giving love away, we receive love. In serving others, we are made whole. In losing our life for Christ, we save it. Palmer details the benefits of leading a God-filled life of work, creativity, and caring:

> Community and individuality are not an either/or choice, any more than life and death are. Instead, they are the poles of another great paradox. A culture of isolated individualism produces mass conformity because people who think they must bear life all alone are too fearful to take the risks of self-hood. But people who know that they are embedded in an eternal community are both freed and empowered to become who they were born to be.
>
> In the active life of work, creativity, and caring we are given endless opportunities to lose ourselves so that we may find ourselves, to join with others in the great community so that, freed from isolation, we may become who we are. . . . [By] joyfully embracing the threat of resurrection we can work, create, and care in ways that take us not toward the futility of death but toward the fullness of new life for ourselves and for the whole of creation.[7]

When I focus on God, my health improves. When I serve others, I am, in fact, serving myself. This game plan has become my calling, my vocation. To paraphrase Derrick Bell, it is the key to my pleasure in life, it is the seat of my power, and it is the root of my sense of agency in the world.[8] And, I've learned that, even in the face of hardships along the way, living the game plan God intends for me is fun! It is fun to do good. It is fun to choose right over wrong. It is fun to be healthy. It is fun to have a close relationship with God. It is fun to have great family relationships. It is fun knowing I am making an impact in my community. It is fun helping my friends. It is fun knowing that I am adding value at work. It is fun taking time to enjoy God's creation. It is fun to sleep well at night. It is fun to be secure in the knowledge that through God's grace and mercy I will go to heaven when I die. Living a life of wholeness simply has no downside.

You and I Will Stay Behind

Several years ago, the Loretto Repertory Theater in St. Louis performed a play called *The Living*, based on a book written almost 340 years ago. Its various chapters were authored by several individuals who lived in London during the Plague of 1665. They were among the few who were brave enough to stay behind to help those who were dying. They found time, out of their twenty-hour workdays, to write their story, knowing it was important to tell their story for, in their words, "you who read this book may learn from our actions, if in your time the plague should come again." During the month of June, during the worst year of the plague, one thousand people died. The following month, the death toll rose to one thousand a week. In August, it was close to one thousand a day, and, for a few days, one thousand people died each hour. Nearly every well person who lived in London fled, including doctors, law enforcement officers, politicians, parents, relatives, neighbors, the king, and almost all the clergy. Even those who were responsible for human care and spiritual nourishment abandoned those in need. Thankfully, a few remained, putting their own lives at risk, to serve those who were dying.

We see the work of such self-sacrificing people still today. The firefighters who rushed into the World Trade Center on September 11, 2001; Todd Beamer and his colleagues on United Airlines Flight 93 that crashed in Pennsylvania that same day; the medical personnel who responded during the SARS outbreak; relief workers who put their lives at great risk in places like Afghanistan, Iraq, Ethiopia, Liberia, New Guinea, and Peru; and our military men and women who are willing to sacrifice their lives in order to protect our freedoms.

There is a sense in which you and I, in choosing to follow God's Game Plan for Life, have also made a conscious decision to "stay behind." Our modern-day plagues have different names and appearances than the plague in the 1600s: AlQaeda, SARS, AIDS, bigotry, selfishness, abuse, neglect, pornography, drought, violence, corporate greed, apathy, pollution. But they are plagues all the same. By choosing to follow God's Game Plan, in our living out of shalom, we have chosen to remain and fight to the finish as we work toward wholeness in our world, our community and ourselves.

Ours Is the First Generation

We are blessed to live in an exciting time in history. We are redis-covering every day—and having confirmed by scientific data—the biblical truth that our physical, mental, and spiritual health are interconnected. This truth impacts our world in significant ways. In the words of Aleksandr Solzhenitsyn:

> We have placed too much hope in politics and social reforms, only to find out that we were being deprived of our most pre-cious possession: our spiritual life. It is trampled by the party mob in the East, by the commercial one in the West. [History] will demand from us a spiritual blaze; we shall have to rise to a new height of vision, to a new level of life, where our physical nature will not be cursed, as in the Middle Ages, but even

more importantly, our spiritual being will not be trampled upon, as in the Modern Era.[9]

Solzhenitsyn captures the fact that we possess the technology and the opportunity to utilize our body, mind, and spirit in active service to our Lord.

God has provided us with the resources. The rest is up to us. We know what it takes: prayer, initiative, and perseverance. God promises to be with you at every turn. Jesus says, "Take my yoke upon you and learn from me, for I am gentle and humble in heart, and you will find rest for your souls. For my yoke is easy and my burden is light" (Matt. 11:29-30). Philip Yancey calls this the "paradox of the yoke." When we follow the Game Plan for Life, Jesus promises the peace of God, which transcends all understanding—"a peace and wholeness in the midst of illness, marriage difficulties, unemployment, terrorist attacks, and the rest of the trials and tribulations we call life."[10]

The Endless Possibilities

What happens when we take these first steps, when we implement the five game plays into our own life? Goethe describes the endless possibilities:

> Concerning all acts of initiative and creation there is one elementary truth, the ignorance of which kills countless ideas and splendid plans: That the moment one definitely commits oneself, then Providence moves, too. All sorts of things occur to help one that would otherwise never have occurred. A whole stream of events issues from the decision, raising in one's favor all manner of unforeseen incidents and meetings and material assistance, which no man could have dreamt would have come his way. Whatever you can do, or dream you can, begin it. Boldness has genius, power, and magic to it.[11]

It is my prayer that you will commit yourself to lead a life of wholeness. God works through our choice to strengthen our family relationships, serve our community, deepen our faith, enhance our congregational life, enliven our witness to others, become healthier, bring forth new ideas, and improve the world for our children and grandchildren. May this book, in some small way, open a window upon the life that God wants you to live—a life of wholeness, a life of discipleship, a life that means joy on earth and the promise of heaven.

Our actions toward this end are a benefit to you and affect all of humanity. J. Heinrich Arnold explains, "And if God's light enters and moves the hearts of just two or three people on earth, it will affect all the rest. It will even affect presidents, prime ministers, generals, and soldiers."[12] All that we will leave behind when we die is what we have done on behalf of others. These persist, and their ripple effect will remain long after we are gone. Our faith in Christ, our witness, our love for others—these are what truly matter. And when you stand before God, your selfless acts made perfect in the light of Christ, God will say, "Well done, good and faithful servant."

Journal Questions—Conclusion

"And what does the Lord require of you? To act justly and to love mercy and to walk humbly with your God."
—Micah 6:8

Is this an accurate summation of the framework of wholeness? Using your own words, develop your own personal mission statement that will assist you in incorporating wholeness into your daily living.

"I don't know what your destiny will be, but one thing I know: the only ones among you who will be really happy are those who will have sought and found how to serve."
—Albert Schweitzer

Create your own action plan on how you will implement the five game plays into your own life. How will implementing this plan add wholeness into your own life?

"In prayer there occurs a turning of heart to [God] who is always ready to give if we will but take what He gives."
—Saint Augustine

What earthly desires and possessions keep you from taking what God wants to give you? Why is it so difficult for us to submit to God's will?

"What is to give light must endure burning."
—Viktor Frankl

What burning have you endured in your life? How have these trials and tribulations prepared you for the life God intends you to lead?

"As long as it is day, we must do the work of him who sent me."
—John 9:4

What work has God asked you to do today? This week? This month? This year? During your life? Create a list of action steps that describes how you intend to accomplish these tasks.

Introduction

1. Billy Graham, *Holy Spirit: Activating God's Power in Your Life* (Nashville: Word Publishing, 1978), 11.
2. Elizabeth Bernstein, "More Prayer, Less Hassle," *Wall Street Journal*, June 27, 2003, sec. W1, 4.
3. Minneapolis: Augsburg Books, 2003.
4. Written correspondence to the author dated May 6, 2003. Christian Harrison left the practice of law and recently graduated from the seminary. Rev. Harrison currently serves as pastor of First Presbyterian Church in Giddings, Texas, continuing to lead a life of significance by helping his members connect their values to their everyday lives.
5. Martin Luther, *The Freedom of the Christian,* as quoted in Garth D. Ludwig, *Order Restored: A Biblical Interpretation of Health Medicine and Healing* (St. Louis: Concordia Publishing House, 1999), 127.
6. Dietrich Bonhoeffer, *The Cost of Discipleship* (New York: MacMillan, 1963), 98.
7. Berkeley: University of California Press, 1985, 7.
8. Wayne Muller, *Sabbath: Finding Rest, Renewal, and Delight in Our Busy Lives* (New York: Bantam, 1999), 2.
9. Kathleen Norris, *The Cloister Walk* (New York: Riverhead, 1996), 63, quoted in Rochelle Melander and Harold Epply,

The Spiritual Leader's Guide to Self-Care (Bethesda, Md.: Alban Institute, 2002), xiii.

Chapter 1

1. Martin Luther, *Heidelberg Disputation,* 1518, in *Martin Luther's Basic Theological Writings,* ed. Timothy Lull (Minneapolis: Fortress Press, 1989), 31.
2. G. Lloyd Rediger, *Fit to Be a Pastor: A Call to Physical, Mental, and Spiritual Fitness,* (Louisville: John Knox Press, 2000), 15-16.
3. John Knowles, "The Responsibility of the Individual," in John Knowles, ed., *Doing Better and Feeling Worse: Health in the United States* (New York: W.W. Norton, 1978), 79, as quoted in Dennis T. Jaffe, *Healing from Within: Psychological Techniques to Help the Mind Heal the Body* (New York: Simon & Schuster, 1980), 10.
4. Uwe Siemon-Netto, "Analysis: Pray Often and Live Longer," *United Press International,* July 23, 2003.
5. Garth Ludwig, *Order Restored: A Biblical Interpretation of Health, Medicine, and Healing* (St. Louis: Concordia Publishing House, 1999), 137.
6. William Watty, "Man and Healing: A Biblical and Theological View," in *Contact,* Christian Medical Commission, World Council of Churches, Geneva, Switzerland (December 1979), 5, as quoted in *Order Restored,* 136-37.
7. Elizabeth Skogland, *The Whole Christian* (New York: Harper & Row, 1976), 3, as quoted in *Order Restored,* 138.
8. "Search for a Christian," Christian Medical Commission of the World Council of Churches (Geneva, Switzerland, 1982), 18, as quoted in Abigail Rian Evans, *Redeeming Marketplace Medicine: A Theology of Health Care* (Cleveland: Pilgrim Press, 1999), 63.
9. John Wilkinson, *The Bible and Healing: A Medical and Theological Commentary* (Grand Rapids, Mich.: Eerdmans,

2002), 7, as quoted in Walt Larimore, *10 Essentials of Highly Healthy People* (Grand Rapids, Mich.: Zondervan, 2003), 29.

10. *10 Essentials of Highly Healthy People,* 29.
11. Ibid., 30.
12. Walter Brueggemann, *Living toward a Vision: Biblical Reflections on Shalom* (New York: United Church Press, 1982), 17-18.
13. Ibid., 15-19.
14. Ibid., 20.
15. Ibid., 20-24.
16. *Order Restored,* 76.
17. William Watty, "Man and Healing: A Biblical and Theological View," *Contact* (Christian Medical Commission, WCC) 54 (1979), 5, as quoted in *Order Restored,* 118.
18. *Order Restored,* 75-79.
19. Ibid., 118.
20. *Redeeming Marketplace Medicine,* 90.
21. Ibid., 68.
22. *Order Restored,* 114-15.
23. Ibid., 73.
24. Ibid., 72-75.
25. Ibid., 109.
26. Matthew Harrison, "Why Do Bad Things Happen?" *Caring,* a newsletter of the Lutheran Church Missouri-Synod World Relief and Human Care (Summer 2003), 6.
27. Martin Scharlemann, *Healing and Redemption* (St. Louis: Concordia Publishing House, 1965), 95-96, as quoted in *Order Restored,* 109-10.
28. *Redeeming Marketplace Medicine,* 70.
29. *Order Restored,* 110.
30. New York: Image Books, 1979, 94.
31. Minneapolis: Augsburg Fortress, 2003, 68.
32. Harrison, "Why Do Bad Things Happen?", 6.

33. Jocelyn Godfrey, "Being Well, Living Well, and Dying Well," *Research News & Opportunities in Science and Theology.*

34. Ibid.

35. *Order Restored,* 199.

Chapter 2

1. *Fit to Be a Pastor,* 13.

2. Ibid., 17.

3. Ibid., 38.

4. *Order Restored,* 128.

5. *Redeeming Marketplace Medicine,* 72.

6. Grand Rapids: Zondervan, 2002, 227-33.

7. *Redeeming Marketplace Medicine,* 72.

8. *Order Restored,* 129-30.

9. Dennis T. Jaffe, *Healing from Within: Psychological Techniques to Help the Mind Heal the Body* (New York: Simon & Schuster, 1980), 5.

10. Ibid.

11. *Fit to Be a Pastor,* 46.

12. J. Heinrich Arnold, *Discipleship* (Farmington, Pa.: Plough Publishing House, 1994), 3.

13. *Order Restored,* 139.

14. *Discipleship,* 253.

15. Ibid., 252.

16. Jean Vanier, *Eruption to Hope* (New York: Paulist Press, 1971), 63, quoted in Arthur Simon, *How Much Is Enough? Hungering for God in an Affluent Culture* (Grand Rapids. Mich.: Baker Books, 2003), 167.

17. John Michael Talbot, *The Lessons of St. Francis: How to Bring Simplicity into Your Daily Life* (New York: Plume, 1997), 228-29.

18. *Discipleship,* 265.

19. *Order Restored,* 130.

20. John Sanford, *Healing and Wholeness* (New York: Paulist Press, 1977), 20, quoted in *Order Restored,* 131.
21. *Healing and Wholeness,* 31, quoted in *Order Restored,* 130.
22. Rick Warren, *The Purpose-Driven Life: What On Earth Am I Here For?* (Grand Rapids, Mich.: Zondervan, 2002), 233.
23. John McCullough Bade, *Will I Sing Again? Listening for the Melody of Grace in the Silence of Illness and Loss* (Minneapolis: Augsburg Fortress, 2003), 94.

Chapter 3

1. Dianne Hales, "Why Prayer Could Be Good Medicine," *Parade Magazine* (March 23, 2003), 4-5.
2. Harold G. Koenig, Michael E. McCullough, and David B. Larson, *Handbook of Religion and Health* (New York: Oxford University Press, 2000), cited in, Walt Larimore, *10 Essentials of Highly Healthy People* (Grand Rapids, Mich.: Zondervan, 2003), 165.
3. Kenneth Pargament, "Research Suggests Correlation between Religion and Well-Being," *Research News & Opportunities in Science and Theology* (July 2001).
4. Redford Williams, *The Trusting Heart: Great News about Type A Behavior* (New York: Time Books, 1989), 201.
5. Ibid.
6. Herbert Benson, with Miriam Z. Klipper. *The Relaxation Response* (New York: WholeCare, 2000).
7. "Analysis: Pray Often and Live Longer."
8. Peter R. Giancola and Emily H. Brechting, "Reliance on God Helps Reduce Teen Drug Use," *Research News & Opportunities in Science and Theology* (February 2003).
9. "Why Prayer Could Be Good Medicine," 4.
10. Ibid., 5.
11. Ibid.

12. Rebecca DiSante, "Cruising the Highway of Health: A Conversation with Walter Larimore," *Research News & Opportunities in Science and Theology* (May 2003), 3.

13. "Why Prayer Could Be Good Medicine," 5.

14. Gary Gunderson, *Deeply Woven Roots: Improving the Quality of Life in Your Community* (Minneapolis: Fortress Press, 1997), 8.

15. Eric Stark, "Religious Struggle May Increase Mortality," *Research News & Opportunities in Science and Theology* (September 2001).

16. Ibid.

17. *Deeply Woven Roots,* 100.

18. Ibid., 100-101.

19. Shelley E. Taylor, *Health Psychology* (New York: McGraw-Hill, 1995), 278, quoted in *Order Restored,* 122-23.

20. Dean Ornish, foreword to *Kitchen Table Wisdom: Stories That Heal,* by Rachel Naomi Remen (New York: River Head Books, 1996), xvi.

21. New York: Alfred Knopf, 1980, 145.

22. Ibid., 149.

23. Douglas M. Lawson, *More Give to Live: How Giving Can Change Your Life* (San Diego: ALTI Publishing, 1999), 43-44.

24. Ibid., 29.

25. Ibid, 19.

26. Ibid.

27. Ibid., 33, 36.

28. Ibid., 24.

29. M. Scott Peck, foreword to *More Give to Live,* xii.

30. Dr. Hans Selye, *The Stress of Life* (New York: McGraw Hill, 1956), 285, quoted in *Order Restored,* 145-46.

31. *Order Restored,* 146.

32. *Kitchen Table Wisdom,* 75-76.

33. *Order Restored,* 146.

34. Adam B. Cohen, "For Health, Focus on the Sunny Side of Life," *Research News & Opportunities in Science and Theology* (June 2003), 6.

35. Gregg Easterbrook, "Forgiveness May Be Beneficial to Good Health," *Research News & Opportunities in Science and Theology* (May 2002).

36. Everett L. Worthington Jr., "Forgiveness in an Unforgiving World," *Research News & Opportunities in Science and Theology* (December 2001).

37. www.forgiving.org/campaign/harness.asp (accessed February 27, 2003).

38. "Forgiveness May Be Beneficial to Good Health."

39. "Forgiveness in an Unforgiving World."

40. "Forgiveness May Be Beneficial to Good Health."

41. Joanna Hill, Robert A. Emmons, David Steindt Rast, *Words of Gratitude for Mind, Body, and Soul* (Radnor, Pa.: Templeton Foundation Press, 2001).

42. "Projects on Gratitude and Success Continue to Generate Data," *Research News & Opportunities in Science and Theology* (July/August 2003), 17.

43. Ibid.

44. C. Michael Thompson, *The Congruent Life: Following the Inward Path to Fulfilling Work and Inspired Leadership* (San Francisco: Jossey-Bass, 2000), 120-21.

45. S. R. Cook-Grueter, "Maps for Living: Ego-Development Stages from Symbiosis to Conscious Universal Embeddedness," in M. L. Commons and others (eds.), *Adult Development,* vol. 2 (New York: Praeger, 1990), 89, quoted in, *The Congruent Life,* 121.

46. J. W. Fowler, *Stages of Faith: The Psychology of Human Development and the Quest for Meaning* (San Francisco: HarperCollins, 1981), 200-201, quoted in, *The Congruent Life,* 121-22.

47. L. Kohlberg and R. A. Ryncarz, "Beyond Justice Reasoning: Moral Development and Consideration of a Seventh Stage,"

in C. N. Alexander and E. J. Langer (eds), *Higher Stages of Human Development: Perspectives on Adult Growth* (New York: Oxford University Press, 1990), 35, quoted in *The Congruent Life,* 138.

48. E. F. Schumacher and P. N. Gillingham, *Good Work* (New York: HarperCollins, 1985), 115, quoted in, *The Congruent Life,* 137 (author's italics).

49. A. E. Bergin, "Values and Religious Issues in Psychotherapy and Mental Health," *American Psychologist* 46, no. 4 (1991), 394-403, quoted in, *The Congruent Life,* 137-38.

50. Ibid., 400, quoted in, *The Congruent Life,* 138.

51. *The Congruent Life,* 139.

52. *10 Essentials of Highly Healthy People,* 64-65.

53. Roger Jahnke, *The Healer Within: Using Traditional Chinese Techniques to Release Your Body's Own Medicine* (San Francisco: Harper, 1997), 189.

54. Ibid., xviii.

55. *Healing from Within,* 27.

56. *Order Restored,* 117.

57. Robert Hahn and Arthur Kleinman, "Belief As Pathogen, Belief As Medicine: 'Voodoo Death' and the 'Placebo Phenomenon' in Anthropological Perspective," *Medical Arthropology Quarterly* 14, no. 4 (1983), 18, quoted in *Order Restored,* 147-48.

58. Paul Tournier, *The Healing of Persons* (New York: Harper & Row, 1965), 185, quoted in *Order Restored,* 149.

Chapter 4

1. Stephen R. Graves and Thomas G. Addington, *The Fourth Frontier: Exploring The New World of Work* (Nashville: Word, 2000), 58.

2. Thomas Addington and Thomas Graves, "Balance: Life's Juggling Act," *Life@Work* (November-December 2000), 40, 43.

3. Ibid., 47.

4. Jim Loehr and Tony Schwartz, *The Power of Full Engagement: Managing Energy, Not Time, Is the Key to High Performance and Personal Renewal* (New York: Simon & Schuster, 2003), 12.

5. Ibid., 13.

6. Ibid., 15-17.

7. Nashville: Word Publishing, 1978.

8. Roy M. Oswald, foreword to *The Spiritual Leader's Guide to Self-Care,* by Rochelle Melander and Harold Eppley (Bethesda, Md.: Alban Institute, 2002), x.

9. *Redeeming Marketplace Medicine,* 166.

10. Ibid.

11. Roland Miller, "Christ the Healer," in *Health and Healing: Ministry of the Church,* ed. Henry Lettermann (Chicago: Wheat Ridge Foundation, 1980), 35, quoted in, *Redeeming Marketplace Medicine,* 166.

12. Parker J. Palmer, *The Active Life: A Spirituality of Work, Creativity, and Caring* (San Francisco: Jossey-Bass, 1990), 122.

13. E. Easwaran, "Working in Freedom," *Yoga International* (May/June 1995), 24, quoted in *The Congruent Life,* 168.

Chapter 5

1. *Caring,* a newsletter published by LCMS World Relief & Human Care (Summer 2003), 9.

2. Arthur Simon, *How Much Is Enough? Hungering for God in an Affluent Culture* (Grand Rapids, Mich.: Basic Books, 2003), 54.

3. A. Roger Merrill and Rebecca R. Merrill, *Life Matters: Creating a Dynamic Balance of Work, Family, Time, and Money* (New York: McGraw Hill, 2003), 106.

4. James C. Dobson, "The Family in Crisis: Interview with James C. Dobson," *Focus on the Family* (August 2001), 4, quoted in, *How Much Is Enough?,* 55.

5. Jay Belsky, "The Dangers of Day Care," *The Wall Street Journal* (July 16, 2003), A14.

6. "Fathers Influence Teens Use of Drugs," *Better Health,* a quarterly newsletter published by the Worker Benefit Plans of the Lutheran Church-Missouri Synod (Summer 2003), 3.

7. *Executive Health*, Lutheran Church-Missouri Synod Health Ministries and Department of Human Resources, February 2001.

8. Sue Shellenbarger, "Move Over, Mom: Research Suggests Dad's Role Sometimes Matters More," *The Wall Street Journal* (June 12, 2003), D1.

9. Arlie Russell Hochschild, *The Time Bind: When Work Becomes Home and Home Becomes Work* (New York: Henry Holt and Co., 1997), as described in Kurt Senske, *Executive Values: A Christian Approach to Organizational Leadership* (Minneapolis: Augsburg Books, 2003), 136.

10. Lee Hardy, *The Fabric of This World: Inquiries into Calling, Career Choice, and the Design of Human Work* (Grand Rapids, Mich.: Eerdmans Publishing, 1990), 117.

11. Ibid., 117.

12. Allan Carlson, "The Natural Family Is the Fundamental Social Unit: A Summons to Create Social Engineering," Speech given at the World Congress of Families II, Geneva, Switzerland, November 15, 1999, quoted in *Life Matters,* 106.

13. *Life Matters,* 108.

14. Patrick J. Schiltz, "On Being a Happy, Healthy, and Ethical Member of an Unhappy, Unhealthy, and Unethical Profession," 52 *Vand. L. Rev.* 871, 910, quoted in Derrick Bell, *Ethical Ambition: Living a Life of Meaning and Worth* (New York: Bloomsbury, 2002), 115-16.

15. "Work/Life Balance: Give a Little, Get a Lot," *Management Review* (October 1998), 6.

16. See generally, *Executive Values,* 132-49.

17. *Life Matters,* 107-108.
18. Stewart D. Friedman and Jeffrey H. Greenhaus, *Work and Family—Allies or Enemies? What Happens When Business Professionals Confront Life Choices* (New York: Oxford University Press, 2000), 13.
19. *Life Matters,* 56.
20. Dobson interview, as quoted in, *How Much Is Enough?,* 54-55.
21. *How Much Is Enough?,* 129.
22. M. Scott Peck, *The Road Less Traveled: A New Psychology of Love, Traditional Values, and Spiritual Growth* (New York: Touchstone, 1978), 23.
23. Sue Shellenbarger, "No Turning Back: Parents Debate Whether They Messed Up Their Kids," *The Wall Street Journal* (July 31, 2003), D1.
24. Dayle Shockley, "What Kids Need from Their Dads," *The Dallas Morning News* (June 14, 2003), www.dallasnews.com.
25. *Deeply Woven Roots,* 95.
26. New York: Basic Books, 1997, 277, quoted in *Deeply Woven Roots,* 26.
27. Conversation with Rev. Daryl Donovan, June 23, 2003.

Chapter 6

1. Billy Graham, *The Holy Spirit: Activating God's Power in Your Life* (Nashville: Word Publishing, 1978), 272.
2. Louis Uchitelle, "Working Families Strain to Live Middle-Class Life," *The New York Times,* September 28, 2000, A-1, quoted in *How Much Is Enough?,* 50.
3. *How Much Is Enough?,* 148.
4. *Kitchen Table Wisdom,* 79-80.
5. New York: Simon & Schuster, 2000, 367.
6. Rochelle Melander and Harold Eppley, *The Spiritual Leader's Guide to Self-Care,* (Bethesda, Md.: Alban Institute, 2002), 182.

7. www.highcalling.org, Weekly Message, June 16, 2003.

8. Madeleine L'Engle, *Walking on Water: Reflections on Faith and Art* (New York: North Point Press, 1980), 23.

9. Paul Althaus, *The Ethics of Martin Luther* (Philadelphia: Fortress Press, 1972), 14, quoted in Lee Hardy, *The Fabrics of This World: Inquiries into Calling, Career Choice, and the Design of Human Work* (Grand Rapids, Mich: Eerdmans, 1990), 54.

10. Philip Yancey, "Living with Furious Opposites," John Wilson, ed., *The Best Christian Writing 2001* (San Francisco: Harper, 2001), 319.

11. Ibid., 320.

12. Ibid., 315-28. Some of these thoughts were inspired by reading Yancey's work.

13. *Living toward a Vision,* 40.

14. Matthew C. Harrison, "Theological and Personal Reflections of Confessional Lutheran Involvement in Neighborhood Renewal." Paper distributed to the Board of Directors of the Lutheran Church-Missouri Synod's Human Care and World Relief Ministries on April 3, 2003, of which Rev. Harrison currently serves as its executive director.

15. E-mail correspondence between Gregory Singleton and the author dated July 26, 2003. Used with permission.

16. E-mail from Shannon Webster in a discussion group, June 22, 2003. Used with permission.

17. Quoted in Philip Yancey, "The Holy Inefficiency of Henri Nouwen," *Christianity Today* 40, no. 14 (1996), 80.

18. Henri Nouwen, *Out of Solitude* (Notre Dame, Ind.: Ave Maria Press, 1974), 32, quoted in *Order Restored,* 93.

19. *Order Restored,* 95.

20. Brett Lawrence, "Starbucks Spirituality," Leadership Journal.net. www.christianitytoday.com, November 14, 2002.

21. *Deeply Woven Roots,* 63.

Chapter 7

1. Gilbert Meilaender, "Divine Summons," John Wilson, ed., *The Best Christian Writing 2001* (San Francisco: Harper, 2001), 207-208.
2. Ibid., 209.
3. Lee Hardy, *The Fabric of This World: Inquiries into Calling, Career Choice, and the Design of Human Work* (Grand Rapids, Mich.: Eerdmans, 1990), 46-47.
4. Charles Dickens, *A Christmas Carol,* (New York: Simon & Schuster, 1967), 52.
5. Quoted in *The Congruent Life,* 40.
6. *The Fabric of This World,* 48.
7. *The Ethics of Martin Luther,* 10, quoted in, *The Fabric of This World,* 51.
8. Dale Hanson Bourke, "A Conversation with David Grizzle," http://www.thehighcalling.org (accessed August 25, 2003).
9. Many of these thoughts were inspired by reading *The Congruent Life,* 14-22.
10. "Divine Summons," 213.
11. *The Congruent Life,* 15-22.
12. Os Hillman, "Are We on the Verge of Another Reformation?" *Business Reform* (May/June 2003), 32.
13. "Labor Letter," *The Wall Street Journal,* August 25, 1987, 1, quoted in, Doug Sherman and William Hendricks, *Your Work Matters to God* (Colorado Springs: Navpress, 1987), 268.
14. Sue Schellenbarger, "An Overlooked Toll of Job Upheavals: Valuable Friendships," *The Wall Street Journal,* January 12, 2000, D1.
15. "Are We on the Verge of Another Reformation?", 32.
16. Ibid., 33.
17. Stephen R. Graves and Thomas G. Addington, *The Fourth Frontier: Exploring the New World of Work* (Nashville: Word Pjjublishing, 2000), 11.
18. Paul Johnson, "Riches Breed Innocence But Not Happiness," *Forbes,* April 14, 2003, 43.

19. Ewald M. Plass, ed., *What Luther Says: A Practical In-Home Anthology for the Active Christian* (St. Louis: Concordia Publishing House, 1959), 975.

20. Ibid., 976.

21. *Ethical Ambition,* 180.

22. *The Congruent Life,* 42.

23. New York: Random House, 2003.

24. Rich Karlgaard, "Money and Meaning," *Forbes,* April 14, 2003, 45.

25. Dallas Willard, "Jesus the Logician," in John Wilson, ed., *The Best Christian Writing 2000* (San Francisco: Harper, 2000), 273.

26. Ibid.

27. Ben Patterson, "Holy War," in *The Best Christian Writing 2000,* 191.

28. Ibid.

29. *The Congruent Life,* 172.

30. David A. Skeel Jr., "The Lessons of Enron," *Books & Culture* (May/June 2002), 24.

31. Robert Simons, Henry Mintzberg, and Kunal Basu, "Memo to: CEO's," *Fast Company* (June 2002), 117, 118.

32. Sheldon Vanuaken, *A Severe Mercy* (New York: Harper & Row, 1977), 85, quoted in *The Fourth Frontier,* 184.

33. *The Congruent Life,* 175.

34. *The Cost of Discipleship,* 98-99.

36. *Sabbath,* 175.

37. Ibid., 205.

38. Susan Pulliam, "A Staffer Ordered to Commit Fraud Balked, Then Caved," *The Wall Street Journal,* June 23, 2003, A1, A6.

39. Parker J. Palmer, *Let Your Life Speak: Listening for the Voice of Vocation* (San Francisco: Jossey-Bass, 2000), 32-33.

40. *Ethical Ambition,* 73-74.

41. "Divine Summons," 212.

42. Larry Woiwode, "The Feeling of Internal Bleeding," in *The Best Christian Writing 2001,* 296.

Conclusion

1. Nicolas Cage, interview, *The Actor's Studio,* Bravo Television Network, May 25, 2003.
2. Gen. 32:22-32.
3. *The Road Less Traveled and Beyond,* 285.
4. *Discipleship,* 19.
5. *Let Your Life Speak,* 71-72.
6. Ibid., 31.
7. *The Active Life,* 156-57.
8. *Ethical Ambition,* 36.
9. *The Congruent Life,* 234.
10. Some of these thoughts were inspired by reading Philip Yancey, "Living with Furious Opposites," in John Wilson, ed., *The Best Christian Writing 2001,* 315, 326.
11. *The Congruent Life,* 157 (authors italics).
12. *Discipleship,* 274.

OTHER RESOURCES FROM AUGSBURG

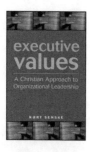

Executive Values by Kurt Senske
176 pages, 0-8066-5153-9 (paperback)
0-8066-4554-7 (hardcover)

This original and practical guide provides Christian leaders with a game plan for Christ-centered leadership that stresses the development of a healthy organizational culture, values-based strategic planning, mentoring, and balancing professional and personal lives

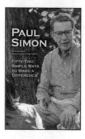

Fifty-Two Simple Ways to Make a Difference by Paul Simon
144 pages, 0-8066-4678-0

A practical and inspiring book for general readers that reminds us that the little things we do count and offers concrete suggestions for small ways of making a difference.

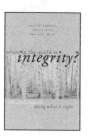

Where in the World Is Integrity?
by Bruce B. Roberts, Craig D. Rice, and Joe E. Smith
208 pages, 0-8066-5154-7

Shares inspiring examples as seen and told by ordinary people. The authors encourage people not only to observe the many acts of integrity around them, but also to discuss what they have observed with friends, family, and colleagues.

Working with Purpose by Jane Kise and David Stark
208 pages, 0-8066-5155-5

Clear direction for using faith as a basic foundation for values and ethics in a secular workplace. Christians in business will learn to identify their own personal and corporate callings in five key areas: purpose, profits, places and products, people, and our planet.

Available wherever books are sold.